War Horse

Nick Stafford's stage plays include *The Canal Ghost, The Whisper of Angels' Wings, Moll Cutpurse, The Snow Queen, Listen with dA dA, The Devil's Only Sleeping, The Go Between, Battle Royal, Luminosity, Love Me Tonight* and *Katherine Desouza*. His plays for radio include *A Matter of Sex* (winner of Sony Gold Award Best Original Script), *Ring of Roses, La Petite Mort, The List, A Year and a Day, The Fire Inside, Birdsong, A Thousand Acres* and *Frankenstein*. His TV films include *The Missing Finger*. His screenplays include *The Blue Suit, Pity* (winner of Dennis Potter Play of the Year Award 1998) and *Katherine Desouza*. He was writer in residence at the Young Vic, 1991, and at Birmingham Repertory Theatre from 1997 to 1998.

Michael Morpurgo is the author of more than a hundred titles. His books have been translated into over twenty-five languages, and many have been made into films and plays. In 1976 he and his wife Clare set up the charity Farms for City Children, and in the last thirty years over sixty thousand children have come to stay and work on one of the farms run by the charity. From 2003 to 2005 Michael became the third Children's Laureate and travelled all over the world telling stories to anyone who would listen. Since then he has continued to write and published ten new titles, among them *Alone on a Wide, Wide Sea, The Amazing Adventures of Adolpus Tips, Beowulf, Born to Run, The Mozart Question* and *Singing for Mrs Pettigrew*.

NICK STAFFORD

War Horse

adapted for the stage from the novel by

MICHAEL MORPURGO

faber and faber

First published in 2007
by Faber and Faber Limited
Bloomsbury House
74–77 Great Russell Street
London WC1B 3DA

Typeset by Country Setting, Kingsdown, Kent CT14 8ES
Printed in England by CPI Bookmarque, Croydon

A CIP record for this book
is available from the British Library

ISBN 978-0-571-24015-9

6 8 10 9 7 5

War Horse was first performed in the Olivier auditorium of the National Theatre, London, presented in association with Handspring Puppet Company, on 9 October 2007. The cast, in alphabetical order, was as follows:

Jamie Ballard **Major Nicholls**
Alice Barclay **Swallow/Emilie**
Jason Barnett **Chapman Carter/Rudi/Heine**
James Barriscale **Sergeant Bone/Colonel Strauss/ Sergeant Fine**
Simon Bubb **Captain Stewart/Soldat Schmidt**
Finn Caldwell **Joey's Mother/Goose/Topthorn/ Veterinary Officer Martin**
Paul Chequer **David/Soldat Schultz**
Tim van Eyken **Song Man**
Thomas Goodridge **Young Joey/Topthorn**
Stephen Harper **Joey's Mother/Dr Schweyk/Coco/ Geordie**
Thusitha Jayasundera **Rose Narracott/Private Shaw**
Gareth Kennerley **Veterinary Officer Bight/Karl**
Craig Leo **Crow/Joey**
Rachel Leonard **Baby Joey/Emilie**
Tim Lewis **Topthorn/Major Callaghan**
Tommy Luther **Joey**
Mervyn Millar **Baby Joey/Emilie**
Emily Mytton **Paulette/Crow**
Toby Olié **Swallow/Joey/Crow**
Toby Sedgwick **Ted Narracott/Coco**
Ashley Taylor-Rhys **Ned Warren/Heine**
Luke Treadaway **Albert Narracott**
Howard Ward **Sergeant Thunder/Soldat Klebb**

Alan Williams **Arthur Warren/Soldat Manfred**
Angus Wright **Hauptmann Friedrich Müller**

All other parts played by members of the company

Directors Marianne Elliott and Tom Morris
Designer/Drawings Rae Smith
Puppet Design and Fabrication Basil Jones and
    Adrian Kohler for Handspring Puppet Company
Lighting Designer Paule Constable
Director of Movement Toby Sedgwick
Music Adrian Sutton
Songmaker John Tams
Music Director Harvey Brough
Video Designers Leo Warner and Mark Grimmer
    for Fifty Nine Productions Ltd
Sound Designer Christopher Shutt
Associate Mervyn Millar

Characters

Joey, a horse

Alice, his mother, a horse

Chapman Carter, auctioneer

Villagers/Ringsiders

Albert Narracott

Ted Narracott, his father

Arthur Warren

Ned, his son

Rose Narracott, Albert's mother

Captain Stewart

Topthorn, a horse

Sergeant Greig

Sergeant Bone

Major Nicholls

Veterinary Officer Bright

Sergeant Thunder

David Taylor

Hauptmann (Captain) Friedrich Muller

Stein, his batman

Gefreiter (Lance Corporal) Karl,
promoted to Offizier-Stellvertreter *

Doctor Schweyk

Colonel Strauss

Paulette

Emilie, Paulette's daughter,
aged seven, aging to eleven

Unteroffizier (Sergeant) Klebb

Schultz

Heine, Coco, horses

Sergeant Fine

Sentry Shaw

Rudi

Schmidt, fleeing German soldier

Geordie

Manfred

Ludwig

Major Callaghan, officer at clearing station

Veterinary Officer Martin

Various soldiers, puppet horses,
other animals and birds

* *Offizier-Stellvertreter:* Acting Officer – a rank (created due to
heavy casualties) given to NCOs who acted in the field as officers
but without the privileges of a commission.

WAR HORSE

Joey – the central character – Alice, his mother, and Topthorn are all horses. None of them speaks but all – especially Joey – have detailed throughlines.

This involves many more stage directions than is normal in a stage play, and these barely indicate the detailed relationships between horse and human that need to be plotted to tell this story. A full description of the horses' movements and reactions would be a script in itself. Therefore what follows is intended to be sufficient to begin.

ONE

Devon – open country, 5 August 1912.

Birds in the sky. Nature at its most natural.

The shape of Alice emerges as she moves.

Joey emerges from behind her. We get to know him.

Joey and Alice stand, heads together. There is intimacy between them.

Joey tries to suckle, three times, but Alice won't let him. Then she turns her head directly towards him – thus Joey is forced away.

Alice leaves him there for a while. Joey is unhappy about this.

Alice changes head angle to let Joey know he can return.

They stay very close, touching, as if replenishing love.

Alice begins to worry. She shows all the signs of trying to locate a sensed threat. Joey picks up on this.

Is the threat from that direction? Or that? Or that? It seems to be all around!

TWO

Continuous.

Enter humans.

They move in towards the horses in a co-ordinated fashion, trying not to scare them.

They form or bring portions of fencing and separate the horses into two pens.

Joey sticks close to Alice. She goes this way, then that, but there is no way to break the pens without using her overwhelming force.

3

She and Joey come to a halt in the middle of the ring of humans.

Suddenly lights come on in the ring and the voice of Chapman Carter, auctioneer, rings out.

Carter Eleven guineas – (*Taking bids.*) Twelve, any advance on twelve? She's worth more than twelve guineas. This is a reluctant sale due to hard times. It could happen to any of you. I'm not asking for charity, just a fair price. Thirteen, thank you. Pay unto others what thou wouldst have paid unto you is all I'm asking. Fourteen, any one? . . . Fourteen guineas for the mare. Fourteen guineas is the best we can do today? Gone!

Enter Albert.

The buyer throws a rope over Alice's head. Joey reacts violently. Humans usher him away from Alice as she is led towards a gap that appears in the ring.

Joey begins to vocalise his distress. Alice answers him.

Exit Alice.

The ring closes behind her. Joey is alone in the ring.

But Alice is refusing to go quietly. She must be controlled before the auction can continue.

Let's get this bliddin' horse moved. Two minutes.

Carter goes to help control Alice. Ringsiders go with him.

Joey runs to and fro.

Albert tries to attract him. Joey faces away from him.

Albert Here, boy. Come on, boy.

Joey seems about to respond when:

Enter Ted, Albert's father, with a pint pot.

Joey's off again!

Ted Eh, Albert, whass goin' on?

Albert Two-minute break, dad.

Ted Oh aye?

Ted watches. There's another moment of contact between Joey and Albert.

Hold me pint whilst I go fer a wotsit.

Exit Ted.

Albert Here boy! Here!

Again it seems that Joey and Albert make contact. Enter Ned Warren at the opposite side of the ring. His abrupt arrival makes Joey take fright. He runs round the ring again.

Here boy, here! Gonna wear yerself out.

Ned That's right, horse, don't pay any mind to him.

Albert ignores him.

Albert Hey boy, hey boy.

Ned Here boy!

Joey definitely favours Albert. Enter Arthur Warren.

Arthur Wassup, Ned?

Ned This foal. Watch him.

Arthur You think he's a prospect?

Ned He's got something.

Arthur He's a hunter, en't he? Half-thoroughbred, half-draught. He's fer riding, so eh, Albert, what would you want with a horse like that?

Ned That your father's pint or are you goin' the same way?

Albert stays focused on Joey.
   Ned deliberately nudges Albert, spilling the pint.

Ned Whoops!

Albert What the –!

Arthur It's for you and yer family's good. We don't think your father should drink so much.

   Enter Ted. The Warrens leave Albert and brush past
   Ted, who retrieves his pint pot from Albert.

Ted Where's my beer?

Albert Ned made me spill it.

Ted He did what?

Albert He nudged me.

Ted Why did ya let 'im do that?

Albert I didn't let 'im.

Ted Eh, did you nudge 'im?

Arthur You talking ta me?

Ted No, ta him.

Arthur There must be sheep for sale, Ned, I can hear one bleating.

Ted Someone owes me a pint!

Albert Dad, leave it . . .

Ted A fresh pint, if you please.

Arthur He (*Albert*) spilled it. Got the Narracott shake.

   Ted goes for Arthur.
   Enter Carter. Ringsiders return.

Carter What's going on?

Ted and Arthur separate.

Two grown men.

Ted One of ya – I don't care which – owes me a pint.

Arthur No.

Ned No.

Carter If you don't mind. Next lot. Hunter colt. Half-thoroughbred, half-draught. His draught mother had a night of passion with a thoroughbred, just like mine did. Looks as if he might have some speed when he gets older.

Ned Buy 'im, vather. He'll be a winner.

Arthur (*to Carter*) We'll have him. Twenty guineas. That's fair.

Carter Twenty guineas bid by Arthur Warren.

There are no other bids.

No? No one else? Going once, going twi–

Ted Twenty-one guineas!

Albert Vather?

Carter Farmer Narracott bids twenty-one? Are you sure?

Ted What d'ye mean, am I sure?

Carter Earlier on you asked me about the calf that's coming –

Ted Changed ma mind.

Arthur Twenty-two.

Ted Twenty-three.

Albert Dad?

Arthur Twenty-four.

Ted Twenty-five.

Albert Dad?

Arthur Twenty-six!

Ted Twenty-seven!

Arthur Twenty-eight!

Ted Twenty-nine.

Albert Dad, we're here to buy a calf –

Ted Dost like the beast or no?

Arthur You can make out through the fug of the ale that this is a horse, Ted? Zot a calf, you know, just 'cos it has four legs and a head.

Ted Twenty-nine!

Arthur Thirty!

Ted Thirty-one!

Arthur Thirty-two!

The Ringsiders know this has got out of hand now.

Carter Gentlemen! Let's take a breath for a moment. And whilst you do that let me remind you that full payment is required as soon as the hammer falls.

Arthur Are you zaying I'm not good for it?

Carter No, Arthur, I am not saying that.

Arthur Then are you zaying Ted Narracott's not good for it?

Ted I'm good for it! I'm damn good for it!

Arthur There's that sheep again!

Ted What was his last bid? What was it!?

Arthur If you're going to bid again, bid thirty-three, thass the next num–

Ted Thirty-three!

Arthur Thirty-four! Thirty-four guineas!

Ted Thirty-five!

Arthur Thirty-zix!

Ted Thirty-zeven!

Arthur Thirty-eight!

Ted If he's good enough for your zon, he's good enough for mine. Think he's gonna ride 'im about the place all la-de-da? Bliddin' Warrens. Thirty-nine guineas!

Beats. Arthur and Ted glare at each other.

Arthur . . . Have 'im.

Ned No!?

Carter Thirty-nine guineas going once . . . Going twice . . .

Arthur Do you have thirty-nine guineas on you, Ted?

Ted begins to pat his pockets.

Carter Gone! Ted Narracott. Thirty-nine guineas.

Ringsiders react.

Albert Dad, you beat him!

Ted Thirty-five pounds.

Albert That's the mortgage money!

Ted Don't tell your mother. Try this pocket. Five pounds, nineteen shillings left ta find.

Albert helps Ted search his pockets.

Albert And here, is this a ten shilling note?

Arthur Na. 'S note from your mother. 'Pay mortgage. Buy calf.'

Ringsiders laugh.

Keep searchin'.

Arthur An' if he does magic thirty-nine guineas then zomeone had better send the doctor round to Narracott's farm, 'cos either poor Rose Narracott's gonna faint when she hears about this or she's gonna give her husband a richly deserved –

Ted I have it! Thirty-nine guineas!

Ned Oh no!

Ted (*to Arthur*) He's mine, that horse is mine!

Ted pays Carter.

Arthur Dunno why you're so happy, Ted. You came to buy a calf and you've paid way over the odds for a fancy riding horse instead.

With little confidence, to the amusement of the ringside audience Ted gets in the ring and cautiously approaches Joey.

Moo!

Ringsiders laugh at Ted's expense.

Albert Vather, let me.

Joey watches Ted put a slip-noose in a length of rope. Ted gets almost close enough to touch Joey, then makes a hash of the last bit, throwing the noose but missing as Joey avoids him and takes fright anew.

Let me do it.

Ted Shut up!

Joey careers round the ring to the cheers and jeers of the ringside audience. Ted makes things worse by trying to chase after Joey.

Ned Your vather's clear and sheer drunk again.

Albert What about your vather – what's his excuse for being like he is?

Joey causes Ted to fall over in the ring. Furious, Ted gets up and whips Joey.
    Albert gets in the ring to intervene.
    Ted whips Albert. The place hushes – you could hear a pin drop.

Ted Get home!

Exit Albert.

Carter Lads!

Several other men enter the ring. In a businesslike fashion they force Joey down to the floor. A harness is fitted and he's let up into Ted's insecure custody.

Arthur Ted Narracott masters his new fancy riding horse!

Ted Say what you like, Arthur; you wanted it, I got it. I won.

Arthur What exactly have you won? Buying 'im is the latest minus entry in the ledger that lists Ted Narracott's vollies. He gets ideas above his station, that's his problem. He's stupid! He thinks he's clever, but he's stupid!

Ted Shut your mouth!

Arthur Very stupid! Very very stupid!

Ted Shut your mouth!

Arthur laughs.

THREE

Narracott's farm.

Rose 'N did ya pay the mortgage?

Ted Shut your mouth.

Rose I said did ya pay the mortgage, 'cos he (*Albert*) won't tell me if ya did . . . I know ya didn't pay the mortgage 'cos ya wouldn't've 'ad thirty-nine guineas cash money ta throw away on this –

Ted If ya know I didn't pay the mortgage, why are ya askin' if I did?

Rose What's your plan, Ted? What's your plan fer this horse an' payin' the mortgage 'cos there's no way of keepin 'im, is there?

   Exit Ted.

(*To Albert.*) Can ya do summit ta quiet that horse!

   Albert tries.

'E's not even a proper farm horse, is he?

Albert He's half-thoroughbred, half-draught – hunter.

Rose I know what a bliddin' hunter is – you, young man, were supposed to be keeping a watch on your vather.

Albert I can't help it. He gives me the slip. What ya doin'?

Rose Smellin' your breath.

Albert I en't been drinking.

Rose Just as well. I can't whop your vather but I can whop you . . . Albert!

Albert Look how he holds his head.

Rose I don't care how he holds his blidding head or any part of him. It couldn't be worse, could it? Damn yer vather. And Arthur. Right, can't sell it immediately 'cos we'd get what, twenty guineas for him? Right, so bring him on.

Albert We can keep him?

Rose Feed him up, then when he's grown, sell 'im. That's our only hope to turn a profit on him, right? 'N you are going to be in charge of bringin' 'im on. That means all chores: feeding, grooming, mucking out, exercise. You – all of it. As fer not payin' the mortgage, I'll have ta think of something. If ya hear strange noises from the house, don't worry, it's me killin' yer vather.

Exit Rose.

Albert (*to Joey*) She's all right. She's my mum, if ya hadn't guessed.

Joey won't let Albert near.

You don't need to fear me . . . When was the last time you were fed? I bet you haven't had a thing.

Joey is tempted by Albert's bucket of feed.
But Joey doesn't come for it because he doesn't like Albert approaching him face on.

Come on, boy.

Albert places the bucket on the floor, but Joey still doesn't like him being face on.

I won't hurt you . . .

Albert picks up the bucket and, at a loss, turns away.
Joey moves in without Albert noticing.
Albert turns back and Joey stops.

Albert offers the bucket, but Joey won't come because Albert's face on again.

I promise I won't hurt you. It's feed, look. Good feed. Mmmm.

But Joey won't come in and he moves if Albert tries to close the distance.

Albert turns away and catches Joey moving in the corner of his eye. He turns back and Joey stops.

Albert tests what happens if he turns away but keeps the bucket available. Sure enough, Joey comes in for the feed.

That's right, fella . . . Good boy, good boy. That was your mother, wasn't it, zold before you? . . . First time away from her, I bet . . . Look at you . . . First time without your mother but you're not alone, zee? I'm here.

Joey shies away when Albert reaches out to touch him.

'Z alright. 'Z alright.

Joey flinches but doesn't shy when Albert reaches out again.

Joey lets Albert place a hand on him. Albert is talking all the while.

There . . . Zee . . . Thass good . . . Good boy . . . What's your name? What d'ye reckon? What shall we caal you? Let me look at you . . . You look like a Joey, to me. Joey, how about Joey? You like the sound of that, Joey? You do like that, don't you? Joey. Joey. Good boy. Joey. Joey. You like that? You like that, Joey? There you go. Joey. Joey. When I call Joey like that, you'll always know it's me, Albert. That's a good start, Joey.

Note: it may be that Albert and Joey also have a call to use in certain situations, or it may be that Albert's various tones of voice and the name Joey will be all that is required.

Joey and Albert play.
They bond.
They fall in love.
They go into the transition from young Joey to grown Joey.
Albert trains Joey to rear up.

And whey-up! And whey-up! And whey-up!

At the top of his rearing up, young Joey makes way for grown Joey, so that when Albert says:

And down.

It is grown Joey whose front hooves hit the ground.

Song: 'Snowfalls' (p. 95).

And time – two years – has passed.

FOUR

Same. It is July 1914.

Albert Good boy, Joey. Good boy.

They play a little more.
Joey learns how to take Albert on his back.

Now, I'm just going to do this . . . Good boy. And this . . . Good boy. And there'll be some weight . . . Whoa – I've backed off, all right? Calm down, Joey. Calm. Right . . . Let's try that again? . . . Good boy . . . There. Zee? Easy.

Exit Joey and Albert at walking pace.
Enter Arthur and Ned.

Arthur Thass Albert, in't it?

Ned It is.

Arthur What's that horse he's on? Is it that bliddin' foal, growed up?

Ned He looks like a proper hunter.

Arthur Let's see how he goes, though. Looks aren't everything . . . Bliddin' hell.

Ned Bliddin' hell.

Arthur Bliddin' hell.

Ned Bliddin' hell.

Arthur Bliddin' hell. We're havin' that horse.

Exit Ned and Arthur.
Enter Albert and Joey.
Joey's as happy as when he was with his mother at the start of the play. It's as if the piece of elastic now joins him and Albert – their symbiotic relationship is complete.

Albert You were born for that, Joey. Born for it. We were born for each other.

Enter Rose.

Rose How's he coming along?

Albert He's not stopped his nipping and he leans on me. Not worth much till that's sorted out.

Rose You sure about that?

Albert Yes.

Rose You see, Albert, I was watching you ride 'im.

Albert Oh.

Rose Well done, Albert. He looks in the peak of health. We'll sell 'im, now. Fetch a good price. You've done well with 'im. Supper's ready.

Exit Rose.
      Albert stables Joey (or a stable forms around them).

Albert I have done well with ya, haven't I? But it means she wants to sell you. To persons unknown. Who aren't meant ta be with ya like I am . . . I'll find a way ta keep ya. I will. I will. I'll find a way.

      Exit Albert.
      Offstage, Arthur has provoked Ted into making a bet.

FIVE

Stables. Night, 29 July 1914.
      Enter Ted, drunk.
      Goose gets involved.
      Ted tries to put a collar on Joey.
      Joey rejects it.

Ted *(to Joey)* Don't mess me about. I'll whop ya till ya bliddin'.

      Ted tries again. He gets the whip and attacks Joey.
      Joey kicks Ted.
      Ted falls to the floor.
      Joey's agitated.
      Enter Albert. He's torn between his father and his horse.

Fetch my gun! Fetch me my gun! I'm gonna kill 'im!

      Enter Rose.

That beast attacked me!

Rose Were you trying ta collar him?

Ted He's got ter plough!

Rose Ted?

Ted Gun or plough! He's got ta plough!

Rose No, he has not. He's a hunter. Albert's brought him on and he's now ready to se–

Ted I've bet that he will plough. In a week.

Rose Bet money?

Ted Money.

Rose With whom?

Ted Who d'ye think?

Rose Oh no.

Ted Arthur.

Rose Oh no. Aaarrrghhh! How much is at stake?

Ted If we win –

Rose We won't win –

Ted Thirty-nine guineas, the price we paid for –

Rose This riding horse will not plough, not in a week, not in a year – it's a ridin' horse, that's its value, so what does Arthur win, 'cos you might as well go and pay up now.

Ted . . . The horse.

Albert No!

Rose What?

Albert What a stupid bet!

Ted Don't talk ta me like that!

Albert Stupid! Stupid!

Ted What have you bin teachin' im? You taught him anything? You've bin in bliddin' charge, haven't yer?

Red mist descends again. Ted approaches Albert. Rose gets in the way, so Ted whops Joey.

You will bliddin' plough. You will –

Rose Ted, please stop –

Ted You will bliddin' plou–

Albert I'll teach him ta plough!

Ted reaches for something more dangerous than his whip.

I'll teach him ta plough!

Ted You'll teach him? An' ya call me stupid? You're the stupid one . . . I'd rather shoot him than let the Warrens have him.

Exit Ted.
Joey becomes readier to be calmed by Albert.

Albert He's drunk, again!

Rose Albert!

Albert Joey can plough in a week?!

Rose Albert –

Albert You agree it's a stupid bet!

Rose Albert, shut up!

Albert He hasn't a chance in hell of teaching him ta plough in a week!

Rose I know –

Albert An' I tell ya, next time he raises his hand ta me or Joey, I'll –

Rose You'll what? What are ya sayin'? What are ya sayin' ya'd do? You makin' a threat? . . . You dare ta

19

whop yer father an' I'll whop you harder than you can bliddin' imagine – ya'll think the sky's fallen on yer head!

Albert If ya hate me so much maybe I should just run away!

Rose Eh?

Albert You always take his side.

Rose No, I don't –

Albert Ya do!

Rose I don't.

Albert Why?

Rose Albert –

Albert I hate him! I'm goin', an' I'm takin' Joey! I'll send ya thirty-nine guineas when I can, then ya won't have ter worry about –

Rose My family didn't want me ter marry yer father, they were against it most strongly, they tried ta stop us, then I . . . They were against us, 'n that's when it started, between yer dad and my brother.

Albert What?

Rose They said he wasn't good enough – they tried ta put a stop to us – but you know what, Albert – they didn't succeed, did they?

Albert What are ya sayin'?

Rose I was carryin' his child – carryin' you.

Albert Oh.

Rose 'Oh' is what yer father said when I told him I was pregnant. But it's not what my family said.

Albert I see.

Rose And you were much, much wanted. Always were, always will be . . . Yer father could've run away when things were that difficult – and they were very, very difficult . . . I often think of my brother as a combination of two birds: an owl that can turn its head right around and watch everything, and a crow with its nasty stabbing beak. Whilst yer father . . . he has trouble in his head. There. Now. Said . . . I've lain awake any number of nights listening to him. He mutters and he moans and I catch the odd word and I think what's he goin' on about? An' after many years of trying ta understand this nocturnal mumble, I think that what he's goin' on about is mistakes. That he's made. Real mistakes. But also imaginary mistakes. My brother has got my husband to believe that he's a failure. I know, I know he drinks. That's a remedy to help him forget his mistakes – and I know the remedy makes things worse because it causes him to make more, worse mistakes. There we are. And Ted Narracott's the head of our farm, our king and our kaiser, and we love him – so me, and you, have ta try ta sort out his mistakes, such as this futile bet with half-owl, half-crow, all bastard brother Arthur. So what ye should do now is spruce Joey up and take him over to yer uncle. That at least will save us the humiliation of – (*losing the ploughing*).

Albert No!

Rose But what else can we do? You said yourself it's impossible.

Albert Can't let him go ta them. I'm gonna try ta teach 'im ta plough – I'm gonna do it – 'n you can't stop me.

Rose . . . All right, you try it. One week. He's a good lad too, really. You're not a bad lad, are you? I know how ya feel, Joey. I could kick Ted Narracott. Next time, Joey, kick him in the head, see if it sorts him out.

Albert Mum?

Rose Yes, Albert?

Albert If we win the bet, can I keep Joey?

Rose That's a big 'if'.

Albert But if I did it, could I keep him? He wouldn't be fer sale any more. He'd be mine.

Rose Perhaps.

Albert And you'd get Dad to agree to that?

Rose I have ta get him ta agree ta let ya plough, first.

Albert Promise.

Rose I promise I'll talk ta him, all right? I really envy you, Albert – your ability ta dream.

Exit Rose.

Albert That was divilish stupid. If you want to survive, Joey, you'll have ta learn that you're never to kick anyone ever again. Mum was joking about next time ya kick vather – no next time! Never kick anyone ever again! Now, I – am going – ta teach you – ta plough – and you – are going – ta learn. Understood? Then we can be together, which is how I believe things are meant ta be. What do you think of that? You believe that, too, don't ya? We got seven days, Joey.

Seven days.

Day one. The collar.

Song: 'Brisk Young Ploughboy' (p. 96).
Joey shies when Albert tries the collar on him.

Stop that! You're just going ta have ta take it. I'm talking ta the draught horse part of ya – the calm, sensible part. Let's try and leave the thoroughbred part of ya out of this.

Joey reluctantly accepts the collar from Albert.

(*Some use of whip.*) Day two. Ploughing bridle and reins. Day three. Today you're going ta pull me, Joey. Now back up? Back up? Day five. The plough. Day seven. You still haven't ploughed yet . . .

SIX

A field. Dawn, 5 August 1914. War was declared by the Prime Minister and Cabinet in London at 11 p.m. on the previous day.

Enter Ned, spying. Goose begins to stalk him.

Joey messes up again.

In a foreshadowing of the episode that occurs later when Joey inspires the gun team, he finds the resources from deep inside to pull the plough.

Albert That's it, dig in, dig in, and pull! And pull! You're getting it, you're getting it. Good boy, Joey! Good boy, Joey! Good boy!

Joey suddenly loses his footing and slips over.

Get up! Get up, Joey! You've got to get up! Joey, you don't know, so I'm going to have to do the knowing for you, that the rest of your life depends on this. So get set to pull straight.

Goose flushes Ned out of hiding.

Albert Spying?

Ned Waiting vor vather.

Albert 'Waiting vor vather.'

Ned I didn't zay it like that, ya little runt.

Albert Runt? It takes one ta know one.

Ned Enjoy your last few minutes with that horse.

Albert 'Waiting vor vather, waiting vor vather.' Thass a runt talking if ever I –

Ned throws himself at Albert. They tussle, then wrestle, inexpertly. To both their surprise, Albert ends up on top, about to whop Ned.

Albert Yes? Yes?

Ned No!

Enter Carter and villagers.

Carter Albert Narracott. Get off him. Bad as yer father.

Albert gets off Ned.
  Enter Arthur, Ted and Rose.

Arthur Let the horse plough straight from 'ere to 'ere.

Ted No, from 'ere to 'ere.

Carter Split the difference.

Ted Agreed. To 'ere.

Arthur That ain't the difference. To 'ere.

Ted To there, then.

Carter Agreed?

Ted You can see my stake, Warren, it's standing there in front of you, but where's yours?

Arthur Thirty-nine guineas. Here.

A cleft stick in the ground. The money in a bag in the cleft.

Rose Good luck, you two.

Joey lines up. Albert cracks the whip but immediately shouts:

Whoa! . . . (*or whatever sound he uses*).

Joey stops.

My vault. My vault. Valse start.

Carter Valse start.

Albert sets everything again and, instead of using the whip, he uses Joey's name and other encouraging sounds, and, with much less struggle than before Joey keeps level and keeps his footing.
Ted and Rose begin to hope . . . The Warrens are incredulous . . . also the villagers.

Rose Come on, Joey, come on, boy!

Ted Good boy, Joey. Good boy!

Albert You're nearly there, Joey! You're nearly there!

The villagers start rooting for Joey.

Rose Go on, go on . . .

Joey succeeds in ploughing the furrow.

Ted Yes! Yes!

Ted snatches the winnings.

Rose Well done! Well done, Joey! And well done, Albert! Well done, both of you.

Ted I won!

Albert gets up on Joey's back and parades victoriously.

Arthur Fluke! Absolute fluke! Clear and sheer fluke!

Rose Not true, Arthur. Albert won fair and square.

Ted Your money in my hand!

A peal of church bells stops everyone in their tracks. Carter takes over.

Carter Listen, everyone, listen! You all know what that means . . . The Kaiser has refused to withdraw his armies from Belgium . . . We are now at war with Germany!

Enthusiastic crowd reaction.

All men in the Yeomanry raise their hands. You men will be mobilised and sent over there with the regular army to sort the Kaiser out and be back in time for tea.

Crowd laughter.

But seriously. Good luck, men. Our thoughts and hearts go with you. And now, more formally, I have to announce that by the powers invested in me I hereby declare that now the British Empire is at war with Germany the government has declared that in the defence of the realm it is henceforth illegal to: keep, carry or fly homing pigeons; fly kites; signal by searchlight and semaphore; display lights, fireworks or fires; and no bells to be rung until the war is ended.

The bells cease.
Exit Carter, leading villagers.

Albert (*to Joey*) Whatever's going on in the rest of the world, you're mine now, Joey, you're mine . . .

Exit Albert and Joey.

SEVEN

Village green, 6 August 1914.
The sequestering and muster – a gathering of men and horses. Military music. Flags. Children with broomsticks playing at marching.
Upstage, Topthorn, bearing Captain Stewart in dress uniform, is serving as the recruiting image.
There are verbal recruiting sergeants directing traffic.

Sergeant Greig Volunteer horses this way, sequestered horses that way.

Sergeant Bone Men with mounts this way, men without that way. Old soldiers up to the age of forty-five this way, new recruits that way.

Sergeant Greig Blacksmiths wanted!

Enter Ted.

Sergeant Bone Surgeons wanted!

Sergeant Greig Horses, fine horses, bring 'em along. Your country needs them, too. And we pay fair. Forty pounds for a trooper's mount, one hundred for an officer's!

Ted How much?

Sergeant Greig One hundred pounds! So if you have a fine horse that you believe deserves an officer on its back, bring it along, bring it along.

Exit Ted.

Sergeant Bone Who wants the King's shilling? (*To Carter and son.*) You take the shilling, I get sixpence – we're both happy. Join up, join up. Enlist here. Attestation forms over there. Over the age of seventeen? Over there. Old soldier up to the age of forty-five? Over here. And repeat after me. 'I swear by Almighty God, that I will be faithful' etcetera, here, you can read the oath on the forms, and add this to it. See, the oath ends, 'So help me God'? Well add this: and God help the Kaiser, because he's gonna need help 'cos we're gonna run him right out of Belgium, right back into Germany, then right through Germany and out the other side, wherever that is!

Enter Arthur and Ned.

Arthur Here, Ned – I've something for ye (*a big knife*). This'uz your grandvather's. He carried it in the zecond

27

Afghan War. And then it uz mine, in the Boer War. We both served to safeguard the Empire and we both survived, and now it's yourn. You look after it and it'll keep you safe. And if you ever have cause to use it, me and your grandvather will be guiding your hand.

Enter Ted with Joey. (They do not meet Topthorn.)

Ted Alright, old zun?

Joey flinches when Ted tries to pat him.

Remember kicking me? Are you Major Nicholls, zir?

Nicholls I am.

Ted I'm Edward Narracott.

Nicholls Volunteering him?

Ted Finest horse in the parish.

Nicholls What's his name?

Ted Joey, zir.

Nicholls Hello, Joey. I've seen you before.

Ted You saw great things, I expect. Officer's horse, I'd say.

Nicholls You would, would you?

Enter Vet Bright. He admires Joey.

Vet Bright No splints, no curbs, good feet and teeth. Sound as a bell. Fit for anything.

Nicholls A hundred pounds, then.

Arthur Eh?

Ted Thank you, sir. Not bad, eh, Arthur? This horse I shouldn't've bought has turned out to be a bit of a money spinner.

Arthur can't conceal his envy as Ted has his hundred pounds counted into his outstretched hand.
Enter Albert.

Albert He's sold him, han't he? He's sold Joey to the army? Joey is my 'orse!

Ted We got a hundred pounds, Albert.

Albert But he's mine! Mum said if I won the ploughin' I could keep –

Nicholls Steady on, young man.

Albert If Joey goes, I go. I'll volunteer.

Ned (*to Nicholls*) He's only just sixteen.

Nicholls You have to be seventeen.

Enter Rose.

Rose Albert?

Albert (*to Rose*) He's sold him to the army –

Ted A hundred pounds, Rose –

Albert You said you'd speak ta him –

Rose I didn't think you'd win –

Albert (*to Ted*) I promise he'll never kick you again –

Ted He's never kicked me –

Albert Yes he did – that means he's not right for the army, don't it? He's got a nasty streak!

Nicholls Young man – come – that's an order. If you ever want to serve you'd better get used to obeying orders.

Albert Sir.

Song: 'Only Remembered' (p. 93).
Freeze except for Nicholls and Albert.

Nicholls Has Joey kicked you? Has he?

Albert . . . No.

Nicholls And has he a nasty streak?

Albert . . . No. He is spirited, but that's the best thing about him.

Nicholls I thought so. Don't worry about your Joey. You've done a fine job on him – he's a fine, fine horse. (*He signals to batman for his sketchbook.*) Have a look at this.

Albert Is that Joey? Is that me? You see him beautiful . . .

Nicholls He'll be my mount. You're helping us bring this war to a swift conclusion by letting us have Joey. Being upset that Joey is going to war is normal, and good. It's understandable if you're worried about what might become of him, just as a parent worries about a son, or a wife about a husband, or a girl about a sweetheart. Am I making sense to you, Albert?

Albert Yes, Major Nicholls.

Nicholls He'll be away a few months at most. The war may well be over before he even finishes basic training – that's three months – then the army will sell him back to you, I'm sure. You have my word as an officer that he'll be well cared for. Doubtless your father was going to ask you if you'd let Joey join up, but as he didn't get the chance, I shall. Will you let him?

Albert Can I say goodbye to him, sir?

Nicholls Of course you may.

Albert (*to Joey*) The thing is, Joey, that you're going to have to go away with that man, Major Nicholls. I want you to do yourself proud. You go and drive those Germans back home, and then you come home. I promise you,

Joey, that we will be together again. We will be reunited. I promise you. You understand that? I, Albert Narracott, do solemnly swear that we shall be together again.

When Joey sees that Albert is leaving he becomes upset. Joey is taken away.

Joey. Joey.

Song: 'The Scarlet and the Blue' (p. 94).

Keep that hundred pounds to buy him back when the war's over. How much will it be to buy Joey back?

Nicholls I can't say, yet.

Albert That money's for Joey.

Exit Albert.

Nicholls He'll come around.

Ted It's good business, Rose.

Rose Your heart must be stone.

Ted We're at war, Rose.

Rose Aren't we just.

Exit Rose.

EIGHT

Military stables. 6 November 1914.

Nicholls (*to Joey*) Training's nearly over but you're not ready for war yet.

Nicholls suddenly fires a round from a pistol near Joey's head. Joey reacts. Nicholls is intending to 'desensitise' Joey – make him used to it.

Good boy. This is a gun. The smell is cordite. Try again.

Fires another round.
  Joey reacts.

Good boy.

  Fires another. Joey reacts.

Good boy, Joey.

  Enter Captain Stewart.
    Nicholls fires two or three rapid rounds.

Good boy. You'll get used to it . . . Imagine if these creatures suddenly evolved – that they became as warlike and violent as us.

Stewart That's an odd thought.

Nicholls You think I'm odd?

Stewart Oh, no, I didn't mean that, I mean I've never thought that about horses.

Nicholls I hadn't until just then. (*Calls.*) Trooper Warren?

  Enter Ned.

Ned Sir!

Nicholls (*to Stewart*) We're posted to France in the morning.

Stewart In the morning it is.

Nicholls Tell the men to stop polishing.

Ned What, zur?!

Nicholls Battle orders; no polishing – buttons, cap badges, buckles, stirrup-irons – let them all go dull. We don't want anything to flash in the sun and give us away. – I know, Warren, after all that hard work.

Ned Sir.

Exit Ned.

Nicholls How's your troop?

Stewart Ready for battle, sir.

Nicholls I was pleased with the practice charge today. Were you and Topthorn far behind?

Stewart We were breathing right down your neck, as you well know. I wouldn't like to be on the wrong end of our charge. My uncle says men tend to go to pieces when our cavalry bear down on them. He's seen men flee or press themselves into the ground. And even if they keep their positions, there weren't many who could face our cavalry and keep their composure – to aim straight as it were. We're going to cut a swathe through Fritz, he won't know what's hit him. He'll wish that he'd never been born, he'll –

Nicholls Well, we're about to discover if all that's true, aren't we? I'm not casting aspersions on your uncle's experience, but every generation has to discover things for themselves, don't they? There's some things that can be understood through telling, but other things have to be experienced before they can be fully apprehended. War is one such thing. How do Joey and Topthorn get on?

Stewart They're a bit snippy, sir.

Nicholls I wasn't imagining it, then. What's that about?

Stewart Two proud animals, sir.

Nicholls Is Topthorn out in the paddock?

Stewart Yes.

Nicholls I'll take Joey out to him. Tell the men to prepare, will you? Reveille at five thirty.

Exit Stewart.

33

The scene becomes a paddock.
Enter Topthorn. Joey and Topthorn react to one another.

Joey, listen. Sort out who's in charge. No fighting – save all that for Fritz . . . You'll be all right, won't you, boys? I just hope that I'm up to it when the time comes. You think I'll be up to it?

Joey and Topthorn are only interested in each other.
Exit Nicholls.

NINE

Same. Continuous.
This is a big moment for Joey – the first time we've seen him alone with another horse since he was separated from his mother. He and Topthorn cautiously explore each other . . . They test each other . . . They compete . . . They play . . . They become friends. Topthorn is the dominant horse – and remains so until Friedrich harnesses them to the ambulance – but the piece of elastic is between them.
Nicholls draws Joey throughout.
Soldiers load Joey and Topthorn . . .

TEN

Aboard ship, 11 November 1914.
Joey and Topthorn, uneasy at their uncertain footing, fail to be comforted by Stewart and Nicholls.
The troopers give up – horses and ships just don't mix – and instead sing a song, perhaps 'It's a Long Way to Tipperary'.

ELEVEN

Quayside, Calais, France, 11–12 November 1914.
   Nicholls leads Joey.
   The sight of soldiers being shipped home upsets Nicholls. Etched on every one of them is wretched misery and pain. There are limbs missing, bloodstains, heads that appear to be incomplete underneath bandages.
   Nicholls has to stop for a moment to compose himself.
   It's uncertain whether Joey puts himself between Nicholls and the men or if Nicholls puts Joey there, but Joey is definitely sensitive to Nicholls' distress.
   Nicholls fusses Joey, as if it's Joey who's upset rather than himself.
   Enter Stewart and Topthorn. Everyone is shocked by the sight of the wounded.

Stewart My God, sir.

Nicholls Don't show any fear or horror, and modify any overt signs of pity. This is normal, from now on.

Stewart Yes, sir.

Nicholls Captain Stewart?

Stewart Sir.

Nicholls Now's the time we must rally the men. Sergeant Greig? Fall the men in by their mounts.

   Bugler sounds commands.

Sergeant Greig Fall in! Stand to your horses!

   The soldiers and horses fall into line.
   They remain until the wounded have passed.

Nicholls We didn't seek this war – the Kaiser unleashed this havoc and his minions, his dogs of war, perpetrated those terrible things on your comrades – the enemy who did that are very near, killing and maiming more of your comrades. They must be stopped, and you are the men to do it! You are the finest soldiers in the finest army on earth! What is more, you have right on your side! So, the task is clear, our motives are the best, and this is the means. You have each a sword, and a rifle, and one hundred and forty rounds. They are swords of justice, and rounds of retribution! A German world? I don't think so, do you? Make the Kaiser rue the day! Let every man do himself, his King, his country and his fallen comrades, proud! Be brave! Fear God! Honour the King!

Troopers Fear God! Honour the King!

Nicholls We are destined to be victorious!

Troopers We are destined to be victorious!

TWELVE

Open country. Next day, 12–13 November 1914.
   Nicholls sees something.
   Bugle call: fall in.

Nicholls (*non-verbal, gestural commands*) Halt! Enemy spotted!

Stewart What is it, sir?

Nicholls Enemy infantry. Open ground. Let's prove your uncle right, Captain Stewart.

Stewart Yes, sir! The men are ready.

   Nicholls gives further gestural commands. The bugler sounds 'fall in'.

Sergeant Greig Stand to your horses! Mount up!

*Everyone knows the drill. They copy when Nicholls
draws his sword and rests the blade on his right
shoulder. When Nicholls advances, they walk in line,
Joey next to Topthorn, rider's knee to rider's knee, in a
phalanx.*

Nicholls Easy, Joey. Easy now, don't get excited. We'll
come through this all right, don't you worry.

Sergeant Greig Advance!

*Nicholls' sword arm extends vertically, ready to sweep
down for the charge (sword pointed at enemy).*
The horses just begin to move.
Incoming enemy machine-gun fire.
*Before they've got going, horses and riders begin to
fall.*

Stewart Where the hell's all that coming from?!

Nicholls Ambush! Machine gun! Break line! Fall back!

Incoming artillery rounds.
Suddenly, Major Nicholls flies from off Joey's back.
Joey's confused.
Chaos.
Nicholls is located in a tree, dead.

THIRTEEN

Behind British lines. Same day.
Ned Warren emerges from the carnage.

Ned Feed the horses. Feed the horses.

Joey and Topthorn are grateful for the feed.
Enter Stewart, and Sergeant Bone with a flask.

Stewart Good lads. Good boys. Rum. Have a shot,
Trooper.

Ned drinks, coughs.

That'll sort you out.

Ned S– sir.

Stewart More (*rum*)?

Ned Y– yes please, sir.

Stewart There's a parcel being got up for home. Anything to go in it?

Ned I don't think zo, zir.

Stewart Trooper Warren? . . . Trooper Warren?

Ned S– sir.

Stewart Are you all right, trooper? Are you injured?

Ned No, sir. But –

Stewart But what?

Ned . . . Those machine guns, sir –

Stewart What about them, trooper? What about them?

Ned Nothing, sir.

Stewart Thank you, Sergeant.

Exit Bone.

Stewart That was a bad start for us, trooper, but we're going to rally and we'll pull through. We'll be going again, and again, until the job's done. It's dog eat dog, them or us. This is war.

Ned Y– yes, sir.

Stewart You know Joey, I think?

Ned A little, s– sir.

Stewart He needs a rider and you need a mount.

Ned S– s– sir?

Stewart You look after him, d'you hear? D'ye hear me? Trooper Warren?

Ned I can ri– ri– ride Joey?

Stewart Pull yourself together, trooper, for everyone's sake.

Ned Yes, Captain St– Stewart.

Stewart Acting Major Stewart. Groom your mount. And stop shaking.

Exit Stewart.
When Ned tries to groom him, Joey finds it irritating at first – Ned is clumsy and unfocused.
Artillery fire in the distance makes Ned twitch. He looks round, ashamed. He notices that the horses haven't reacted badly towards him. He thanks them.

Ned What d'ye think – eighteen-pounders?

He extends his arms and watches them shake.
The chatter of a machine gun makes Ned duck to the ground, sheltering under Joey.
Joey just lets Ned be.
Ned stays as long as he needs to recover.
Ned resumes grooming, less shakily.

. . . You could mow a field of hay with one of those machine guns . . . All the stalks of hay in a field, flat. Rat-a-tat-a-tat flat . . . (*He seems to get stuck for a few moments, only able to rock.*) D'ye think this landscape once looked like home? . . . I wish I hadn't thought of home. Blighty . . . Blighty Blighty. Blighty Blighty Blighty. Zee this (*his knife*)? Cut your hand off – cut your foot off – cut an eye out, go home . . . Anything to put in a parcel for home? Me.

Ned sinks to the ground.
  A battle erupts overhead, but he doesn't react.
  Joey and Topthorn move in and shelter Ned.

FOURTEEN

Farm, Devon. Christmas Day, 1914.
  Enter Ted, pushing a secondhand bicycle with a ribbon tied to it.
  Enter Rose, leading Albert, hands over eyes.

Rose You can look, now. Happy Christmas, Albert.

Albert (*to Rose*) . . . A bicycle. Thanks.

Rose Vather fixed it up.

Albert (*to Rose*) It's grand. No, really, it is. I'll ride it.

Rose That's the general idea . . . I know the Christmas present I'd like – you two to break your silence.

  Beats.

Albert (*to Ted*) . . . You didn't spend any of Joey's money on this, did you –?

Ted There's no such thing as 'Joey's money', it's all one pot –

Albert He'll be back soon, you know, the war must be about over –

Ted If he doesn't kick someone –

Albert He must have had a reason ta kick ya –

Rose Stop! I'd rather have the silence than that bickering.

  Enter Arthur, with a parcel.

Oh . . .

Arthur Yes, um, I was in the post office, in the village, last night, just as it was closing, and while I was there, it happened that there was a parcel for Albert, from the, from the, from over there, and I thought, I could go up that way in the morning, so I offered, and it might not get there otherwise, so I asked if I could, and here it is.

Rose Happy Christmas, Arthur.

Arthur Oh, um. Happy Christmas.

Albert Who's sending me a parcel from over there?

Rose Open it and see.

As Albert does so:

Heard from Ned?

Arthur Yes. Um, not for a while . . . There's been one or two notifications received yesterday. Telegrams, informing, you know . . . on Christmas Eve – terrible.

Ted Papers zay it's going according to plan –

Arthur I'm not zaying it's not. I'm right behind our boys.

Ted We shall prevail.

Rose (*aimed at Ted*) You've fought in a war, haven't you, Arthur?

Arthur In my day they didn't have these machine guns we've been hearing about.

Albert Oh . . .

Rose What is it?

Albert Major Nicholls' sketchbook. Here's his picture, of Joey and me.

Rose Well I never. Of you and Joey?

Albert And there's a letter.

Rose What's it zay?

Albert begins to read.

What's it zay, Albert?

Albert Oh no –

Rose What?

Albert 'Dear Albert Narracott, Major Nicholls, who died in action today, left you this. Yours, (Acting) Major Stewart.'

Arthur Erm, I wouldn't have brought it if I'd –

Rose You couldn't have known it was bad news.

Arthur I'll, er . . . I'll, er, be on my –

Rose D'ye have to go straight away? Come into the house for a cup of tea.

Arthur A cup of tea? Me?

Rose We were about to have one.

Exit Ted.

Arthur Not exactly friends, are we?

Rose You bliddin' men . . .

Exit Arthur.

Albert . . . Major Nicholls was riding Joey.

Rose Whatcha say?

Albert When he died, he was –

Rose You don't know he was riding him when he –

Albert 'In action', it zays –

Rose We'll have to wait and see –

Albert More waiting!

Rose Can ye just shut up about yer bliddin' horse!?

But then Rose envelops Albert in her arms. They stay like this for a while.

He might be all right . . . Tea and cake, all right?

Albert Mum?

Rose What, son?

Albert I do like my bicycle.

Rose Your father put his love into it . . .

Exit Rose.

Albert Well, then . . . Come on, Albert, come on, lad.

Albert tears Joey's picture out and discards the sketchbook.
Exit Albert, on his bicycle.
Enter Rose.

Rose Eh, Albert; I've a small gift for you as well, only a silly – (*She finds sketchbook with page torn out.*) Albert? Albert? . . . Albert! Albert! Ted! He's gone! Albert! Albert!

FIFTEEN

Behind British lines. Beginning of March 1915.
Ned checks his weapons for the umpteenth time: sword, ammunition bandoliers, rifle.
Joey and Topthorn get a whiff of trouble.

Ned Nothing to worry about. Our guns are going to destroy their machine guns, and blow a hole in their wire. Then we're off.

43

Ned fusses Joey and Topthorn.
  Enter Stewart. He gives Ned a swig of rum.
  A deafening barrage starts up, startling the horses.
It's an effort for horse and man not to flinch or, worse,
flee. It's not clear which mammal is comforting which.
There's a channel of comfort passing between man and
horses.
  Stewart signals to bugler.
  Bugler sounds 'mount up'.
  Stewart and Ned mount up.
  Enter the rest of the mounted.

Stewart Our guns have destroyed their wire! Fritz is
there for the taking!

They wait . . .
  The barrage ceases . . .
  Stewart draws his sword. The men copy him.

The time has come when we shall send Fritz back to
Germany!

Troopers Send Fritz back! Send Fritz back! Send Fritz
back to Germany!

Bugler sounds commands: 'Advance.' 'Trot.' 'Gallop.'
  Stewart makes the C.O.'s signal – sword vertical
held high.
  Bugler sounds: 'Charge!'
  Stewart, then the men, sweep their swords down to
point at the enemy.

Stewart Chaaaarrgge!

Troopers Chaaarrrghhhh!

For a few moments horses gallop freely, then the
enemy guns start up. The men use their battle cries to
whip themselves into a frenzy.
  Incoming shells and machine-gun fire create havoc.
Horses rear. Men scream.

44

The ground erupts, throwing horses and men into the air.

Joey and Topthorn keep going.

Ned Our vather which art in Heaven! Hallowed be thy name! Thy kingdom co–

Horses begin to run into the barbed wire. They scream. They become stuck.

Stewart Keep goiiiiing! Attack! There are gaps in the wire! Fritz is there! Fritz is there! Attack through the gaps in the wire! Attaaaaaaaack!

Obeying, Joey and Topthorn leap out of sight.

Interval.

SIXTEEN

Quayside, Calais. Beginning of March 1915.
   Enter infantry privates, including David. Enter Albert, in Yeomanry uniform.
   Enter Sergeant Thunder.

Sergeant Thunder Platoon fall in!

   All the infantry obey. Albert is adrift.

Stand at ease. Bonjour, mes amis! Spring is in the air. Shame you're not on your holidays. Biarritz is very pleasant at this time of year, I'm told. But you're not headed there, and neither am I, more's the pity. Oy, you! Name?

Albert Trooper Narracott, Zergeant.

Sergeant Thunder Trooper Narracott . . . (*Finds him on the list.*) Ah yes. New orders. You're joining the infantry.

Albert Sir?

Sergeant Thunder Don't call me sir, I'm not an effing officer – I work for a living! Hang about – how old are you?

Albert Eighteen . . . Sergeant.

   Sergeant Thunder stares at Albert. Albert doesn't wilt.

Sergeant Thunder More like sixteen . . . You've been effing transferred, Private Narracott who claims to be eighteffingteen, because the Yeomanry mob you were to join doesn't exist any more.

Albert Don't exist?

Sergeant Thunder Correct, so you're now to be a private in the infantry.

Albert What about the 'orses? My 'orse is with that Yeomanry, ee's called Joey, this is his picture –

Sergeant Thunder You have a picture of your horse? Why didn't you say? Ah yes, a simple sketch but unmistakably – what did you say his name was?

Albert Joey.

Sergeant Thunder . . . I don't know where your effing Joey is! Do I look like I know the latest on every effing 'orse in the war? Do I look like an effing equine expert or even an effing equestrian enthusiast? Your mob no longer exists. Any survivors will have been absorbed into –

Albert So there were survivors –

Sergeant Thunder Silence, Private! . . . Are you silent, now?

Albert Sergeant!

Sergeant Thunder You just spoke!

Albert Sergeant!

Sergeant Thunder You just spoke again!

Albert bites his tongue. David's caught smiling.

You! Get here now! And what's your name?

David Private Taylor, Sergeant.

Sergeant Thunder This one seems to think he's on a mission for the Dumb Animals' League, he thinks he's here to nose for his nag, but you know what we're here for, don't you, Private Taylor?

David To win the war, Sergeant.

Sergeant Thunder That's right, you've come to France to kill Germans. Either of you speak French? . . . I'll learn you some. Repeat after me: je suis un bloody sod, je suis un bloody bastard.

David repeats. Albert repeats.

Sergeant Thunder Now take a shovel each. You think I'm joking? Oh, you're going to need your shovels, boys – move! Here's another French word for you to learn: impasse. And another: dig. And another: trench. Six months we've been here, and we may be another six before it's over, so we're making ourselves comfortable. Attention. Right turn, toot sweet to the front; and the tooter the sweeter! Now quick march, to the tune of 'Dolly Gray'.

Song: 'Dolly Gray' (p. 98).

Exit Albert and David et al.

SEVENTEEN

Stewart and Ned.
German soldiers guard them. One of them is Karl, a Gefreiter (Lance-Corporal). Another is Stein, Friedrich's batman.
Hauptmann (Captain) Friedrich Muller shoots British horses trapped on the wire.
When he nears, the German soldiers defer to him.

Friedrich Major . . .

Stewart Hauptmann.

Friedrich *Der Angriff war Wahnsinn.* [That charge was folly.]

Stewart I don't speak Fritz, Fritz.

A nod from Friedrich and the German soldiers search Stewart and Ned. Ned resists.

Trooper Warren!
Let them search you. We're prisoners of war, now.

The German soldiers – Karl especially – are agitated.

Ned It was my vather's!

Stewart Give it to them!

Then Ned has the knife in his hand, threatening.

Karl kills Ned. It's very brutal – and possibly involves Ned's knife used against him.
    Joey reacts. Friedrich tries to placate him, speaking English.
    Karl turns on Stewart.

I'm unarmed! I've no concealed weapons!

Friedrich (*to Karl*) *Genug, Gefreiter, er sagt dass er unbewaffnet ist!* [Enough, Corporal, he's saying that he's unarmed!]

Karl obeys.

That is what you were saying, Major, that you're unarmed? You may not speak Fritz, as you say. But some of us speak Tommy, Tommy.

Enter Joey and Topthorn, in distress, led by a German soldier. Friedrich fusses them.

Beruhigt euch. [Calm down.] What beautiful creatures, Major. Easy. What are these horses' names? Tell me their names. No? Look into his eyes. The Gefreiter's comrades are all gone. Killed by an English shell. He's out for blood. I'm glad I'm on his side.

Karl knows he's being talked about in English and he doesn't like it.

Karl *Entschuldigung, Herr Hauptmann, was sagen Sie?* [Excuse me, Captain, what are you saying?]

Friedrich Shall I let the Lance Corporal escort you alone?

Stewart . . . Topthorn, Joey.

Friedrich gestures to soldiers, who surround Stewart.

Friedrich Topthorn. Joey.

Karl *Sie sprachen Englisch mit den Pferden?* [You are speaking English to the horses?]

Friedrich *Fuhren Sie ihn weg. Und tun Sie ihm nichts an.* [Take him away. And don't harm him.]

Karl *Hauptmann.* [Sir.]

Stewart Goodbye, Topthorn. Goodbye, old lad.

Exit Stewart, under guard.

Joey and Topthorn display anger and distress. Friedrich expertly calms them.

Friedrich (*English*) Calm down, Joey. Topthorn. Ah. Does that make you feel like home? I tell you, if we had one jot of the courage of you animals . . . You are like my Siegfried. Shrapnel passed through his brain, snipped the corner of my head. Phut, down he went. You were lucky. And now, my friends, you will be joining the German cavalry so that you can ride into the English machine guns. And I will be going with you. You know what it's like out there. How long do you think we will last?

Enter Colonel Strauss and Doctor Schweyk.

Dr Schweyk (*covered in blood*) *Dieser Hof wird eine Durchgangstation. Wir bauen einen Krankenwagen. Wir versammeln die Verwundeten hier und bringen sie zum Spital.* [The farm is to be a clearing station. We're making an ambulance. We collect the injured from here and take them to the hospital.]

There are soldiers adapting a farm cart, marked with a prominent red cross.

Strauss *Herr Hauptmann? Kann man diese Pferde an so einen Wagen anspannen?* [Can you harness this cart to these horses?]

Friedrich *Herr Oberst, diese Pferde können den Karren nicht ziehen, der eine ist ein Vollblut und der andere ein Jäger –* [Colonel, these horses won't be able to pull a cart, they're a thoroughbred and a hunter –]

Strauss *Tun Sie es einfach. Morgan können Sie zurück zu ihre Einheit.* [Just do it. You can rejoin your unit tomorrow.]

Friedrich *Hauptmann.* [Sir.] Another impossible thing for you to do, boys. If you pull this ambulance, you won't be charging into the English guns tomorrow. I know. I know. He might as well ask me to pull it. You've probably never seen one of these things, never mind worn it. But it might save your life – for a bit. I wish I could make you understand. Come on, Topthorn.

Friedrich tries to harness Topthorn to the cart. He fails. Friedrich has to placate Topthorn.

Friedrich *Tut mir leid.* [I'm sorry.]

Dr Schweyk *Also werden die Verwundeten sterben?* [So the wounded will die?]

Song: 'Brisk Young Ploughboy' (p. 96).

Friedrich *Das sind die falschen Pferde.* [They are the wrong horses.]

Friedrich tries with Joey. Success!

Was? [What?]

Dr Schweyk *Sehen Sie! Sie wissen ja gar nichts über Pferde!* [See! You don't know anything about horses!]

Friedrich (*to Joey*) You've done this before? To use a beautiful hunter like you as a carthorse. Now I know the English are mad.

Schweyk leads Topthorn. Yes, he will comply now that Joey's led him.
Enter Paulette. She'd like to pass unnoticed.
Another soldier demands Paulette's papers. These have been issued by the occupiers and she needs them to move any distance at all. She effectively has to carry a passport, and also formally apply to travel longer distances than the everyday.

Walter *Papiere!* [Papers!]

Dr Schweyk (*scribbling receipt*) *Wir brauchen ihren Karren . . . verstehen Sie? Das. Das hier. Wir nehmen das.* [We need your cart . . . Do you understand? This. This. We're taking this.] *Madame, nous besoin ça . . . Ich weiss das Wort nicht.* [I don't know the word.] *Nous besoin* this.

Paulette *Je fous ça avec toute la paperasserie de merde.* [I'll put it with all the other useless bits of paper.]

Exit Paulette.

Dr Schweyk *Sie, Hauptmann. Spannen Sie bitte das andere Pferd ein und fahren Sie diesen Krankentransport zum Spital.* [You, Hauptmann. Please harness the other horse and drive this ambulance to the hospital.]

Friedrich *Ich?* [Me?]

Dr Schweyk *Ja. Sie haben den Oberst gehört. Morgen können Sie zurück zu ihre Einheit. Befehle.* [Yes. You heard what the Colonel said. You can rejoin your unit tomorrow. Orders.]

Joey encourages Topthorn. Joey is taking over as the dominant one.

Friedrich (*to Topthorn*) So I rejoin my unit tomorrow.
Come on, Topthorn. Now your friend's shown you how.
Ambulance driver, ambulance horses. What is the world
coming to? There, boy, there. You're a full thoroughbred!
Men are dying out there so you must pull this ambulance.
Don't worry; I shall look after you. And Joey will look
after you. Joey, you must show Topthorn how to do this.
I understand what you horses have been through. I never
imagined that something I could not see – had no warning
of – could slice my Siegfried, sunder him – phutt! I could
see his insides. How do you become accustomed to seeing
insides? Siegfried split in two under me. His head sliced
down the middle and for an instant he had two mouths
facing opposite directions and both his eyes looked back
at me. Like this shape. In front of me. (*A gesture with his
hands.*) 'Siegfried' means victory.

> *Paulette hurries back through, holding her papers aloft
> as if to say, 'Yes, yes, I do have some.'*

Play your cards right and you may stay with this
ambulance, and that way keep out of the fighting. Me?
I'll have to rejoin the cavalry.

> *Wounded bodies are put on the cart.*
> *Friedrich urges Joey and Topthorn towards the
> hospital.*
> *Joey leads the way.*

EIGHTEEN

*A shallow crater in disputed territory. Beginning of
March 1915, following a successful surprise German
attack.*

*Albert dives in, closely followed by David. They scan
the horizon. Nicholls, dead, appears on the edge of this
scene.*

Albert Fritz your way?

David No. Yours?

Albert No. We're right in it.

David Where did they come from?

Albert First I knew, they were in our trench. The only English I heard was, 'Fall back! Fall back!'

David What shall we do now?

Albert Why are you asking me?

David I followed you 'cos I thought you knew what you were doing.

Albert I was just shitting myself, Private. Just shitting.

David Are we the only ones who made it?

Albert Can't be.

David Might be.

Albert Can't be.

Beats.

David Shall we make a run for it in the dark?

Albert But we're lost, so which way?

David . . . Dunno.

Albert We could be running towards them.

David Come on, Albert. You're the country boy, you're the one who buggers about in fields at night.

Albert Nothing to see, is there? Nothing. No stars, no moon . . .

David Nothing.

Albert We need four of us to cover all the angles.

David . . . Got any water?

Albert A drop. (*He shares it.*)

David Bon . . .

Albert Bon, indeed.

David If we're gonna run for it, we should run in the dark.

Albert Run in the dark, run into Fritz. Wait for day, Fritz'll see us. We might be behind their new lines now.

David has another look.

I don't think we should look. Better to listen.

Beats.

David We're buggered, aren't we?

Albert We can't be the only ones alive.

David . . . I'm gonna finish a letter to my girl –

Albert Now?

David Will you –

Albert Yes –

David See it gets –

Albert Yes –

David If anything happens to –

Albert Shut up! Nothing's going to happen . . . Your pencil's scratching . . . Hang about.

They listen. They look. Nothing.
Dead Nicholls passes them

David You gonna write to your horse?

Albert Tres funny.

David Can he read? . . . Your silence reveals that the answer to my question is neeeeeigh.

Albert Is that your girl's picture?

David That's her. That's my Flossie.

Albert At least Joey's meant to look like a horse.

David If Flossie's got a long face it's because she's missing me giving her a rub down after a gallop. She's what keeps me going . . . When I was climbing out of our trench I put my hand in something, Albert. I think it was a bit of a man.

Albert It might well have been, Private.

Beats.

David And I've a little brother, Alfie. Promised to teach him to ride a bicycle.

Albert Has he got a bicycle?

David No, but I'll get him one.

Albert I've a spare bicycle. It's in Exeter. I won't need it 'cos I'll find Joey. Alfie can have it.

David Thanks, Albert. That's bon.

Albert 'S all right.

David What is it?

Albert Nothing. Thought I saw something. I will find Joey.

David What?

A German soldier falls into their crater, as surprised as they are.

German Soldier *Her! Her!*

To Albert's surprise, he shoots the German before the German shoots him.

Albert Jesus!

David Now we're for it.

They come under attack. It starts a battle.

Albert That way! I think that's our lot!

David Yeah?

Albert Whadda you think?

David I think so . . .

Albert Ready?

David Ready.

Exit Albert and David.

NINETEEN

Paulette's farm. Beginning of March 1915.
Enter Emilie. She scavenges among the dead. She hears Friedrich, and hides.
Enter Joey, Topthorn and Friedrich, plus bodies on cart. They're completing their first trip from the hospital. Friedrich is still in his cavalry uniform but it's battered and bloody. There's one live soldier – Stein – making a noise.

Friedrich *Sshh, ruhig. Der Doktor ist hier.* [Sshh, now. The doctor is here.]

Friedrich discovers the bodies of Schweyk and others.

Oh? . . . (*He calls.*) Hello? . . . Hello?

Stein makes more noise and dies.

Stein? Nein! Nein! Scheisse . . . Ist jetzt jeder tot? [Stein?
No! No! Shit! . . . Now everyone is dead?] (*He calls.*)
Hello? . . . Hello? . . . Just us, then. And ghosts.

Friedrich shows the horses dead men's effects.

Johann Schnabel. Twenty-one. Photograph of mother and
father. Dr Wilhelm Schweyk. Photograph of wife and five
children. Five! Friedrich – same as me – Friedrich Kroll,
thirty-five. Photograph of wife and three children. Do
you know about death? What do horses think about
death?

Joey discovers Emilie.

*Ist schon gut, kleines Mädchen, ich tue dir nichts. Lebst
du hier? Ich versuche mal Französisch zu sprechen.* [It's
all right, little girl, I won't harm you. You live here? I
shall try to speak French.] (*Primitive.*) *Où est ça père et
mère? Tu comprends? Ça père? Ça mère? . . . Tu est
français? Tu est français?*

Emilie Oui?

Friedrich *Francais, bon. Je parle un petit peu. J'ai un
petite fille. Gisa. Ma fille est Gisa. Tu est? . . . Qu'elle est
ça nom? . . . Ist egal.* [No matter.] *C'est pas important.*
Topthorn, Joey, have you said hello to the little French girl?

Enter Paulette.

Paulette Emilie!

*Paulette protects Emilie from Friedrich while fearfully
offering her papers.*

Friedrich *C'est pas un problem, madame. Les animaux et
mois aime le petite filles.*

Exit Paulette and Emilie.

Oh well. Can't blame her too much, eh boys? We have
invaded their country and made it part of ours – part

58

of mine, that is. But only because they were about to attack us.

But oh, boys, that little girl reminds me so much of my daughter, Gisa . . . Look, here I am. Friedrich Muller, aged thirty-nine, not yet a ghost, photograph of wife, and daughter, Gisa . . .

Shall I tell you a secret? When I was fighting, I didn't know what I was doing. My bowels opened. I was terrified. No – there's a place beyond terrified, and I was in it. Three years training in the cavalry, five years in the reserve, all my life preparing to serve the Kaiser, riding my big, beautiful horse into battle and I was useless . . .

I fear that I'm a coward! Please, please do not tell anyone I said that. Please! But I don't want to die like my Siegfried. I want to see my little Gisa again. Is that cowardice?

You could come home with me, you horses – you want to come to Germany? Back to Schleiden – it is not far, just the other side of Belgium. When this is over?

I wish it were over now. I might rather kill myself than go into the fighting again. How stupid is that? Dying like these men is so awful that I might rather kill myself? You heard the wounded men, you heard the noises they made before they died. I'll be fighting again tomorrow.

There's no one about, there's no one watching me – I tell you, in the army, someone is always watching you, someone always knows where you are, but just at this moment no one does! When I rejoin the cavalry someone will always know where I am again.

So, shall I – what about this for a plan – shall I stay with you? That's a good plan, *ja*? We've done good with this ambulance cart, haven't we? And we could do more! It's an important job, *ja*? What use am I in the fighting if I'm a coward? Cavalry is no use in this war – not with machine guns and barbed wire and trenches. We can win the war without useless me.

He takes succour from the fact that the horses don't contradict him.

Look, my uniform, it is all battered about. I need a new one, don't I? This poor man (*Stein*) – he's about my size, *ja*?

Again, the horses don't disagree.
Friedrich takes the dead private's uniform and puts it on, removing the insignia, adding his Red Cross arm bands.

But I'll be reported dead. Back at home they will think I am dead – can I tell them I'm not? . . . No, they're just going to have to think that I'm dead for a few weeks until this war is over . . .

Will this work, will it? This camouflage, this coward hiding right under the nose of the war. This deserting without actually leaving? . . .

Enter Sergeant Klebb.

Sergeant Klebb *Soldat!* [Private.]

Friedrich ?

Sergeant Klebb *Soldat!*

Friedrich *Ja, Herr Unteroffizier!* [Yes, Sergeant!]

Sergeant Klebb *Wo ist der Doktor?* [Where is the doctor?]

Friedrich *Tot, Herr Unteroffizier.* [Dead, Sergeant.]

Sergeant Klebb *Sind alle tot?* [They all dead?]

Friedrich *Ja, Herr Unteroffizier!* [Yes, Sergeant!]

Sergeant Klebb *Gab es einen Kavallerie-Hauptmann Muller?* [Was there a cavalry captain Muller?]

Friedrich *Der starb da drüben.* [He died over there.]

Sergeant Klebb *Begrabt sie da drüben.* [Bury them.]

Exit Sergeant Klebb.

Friedrich (*busy with horses and cart*) Was there a cavalry captain Muller? There was. Ambulance cart, ambulance horses, ambulance orderly until the end of the fighting – let's pray for an even swifter victory than the Kaiser promised, then home, home to little Gisa.

TWENTY

Narracott's farm. Early August 1915.
   Ted works.
   Enter Rose, with a letter.

Rose Ted. It's a letter from our boy.

Ted What does it say?

   Friedrich continues dragging bodies past Ted into the gloom.

Rose 'Dear Mother. Please don't be angry with me for running away. I am all right. The sun is shining today. I've found a good chum called David. And they've made me a Lance Corporal. Horse in French is *shove-oh. Ju shursh* Joey means I look for Joey.'

Ted They could have sequestered that horse for less money – forty pounds – and I would have been helpless to stop them and then I wouldn't be getting the blame for Albert goin' off because I sold the horse that kicked me.

Rose I wish it was you over there, not him. He's just a boy.

Ted turns away. Rose continues reading.
   Emily emerges to help feed Joey and Topthorn

'You're a *bon* mother . . .' *Bon.* 'And I am eating enough.
Not like your own food, of course.'

   Song: 'Snowfalls' (p. 95).

Friedrich and Emilie continue.
   David and Albert can be seen cleaning their guns.
   Snow falls on stage

David We'll be going over (*the top*) today, do you think,
Albert?

Albert Keep cleaning your rifle and it will never happen.

David Yes, Lance Corporal.

Albert Albert to you, Private.

Rose 'We're in farmland. What used to be farmland.
I think it was always flatter than home is, but it's been
knocked about a bit. Don't worry, everything will be
back the way it was, soon –'

Albert David?

Rose Ted? Ted?

Albert Come on. It's a no-show day, today.

   Song: 'Snowfalls' (p. 95).

   Exit David and Albert. Exit Rose.

TWENTY-THREE

Paulette's farm. Xmas 1916.
   Enter Karl (now with rank of Offizier-Stellvertreter),
pulling two knackered horses, Heine and Coco, pulling
an artillery piece.

Karl *Zieht! Zieht! Kommt schon ihr Viecher. Zieht!*
[Pull! Pull! Come on you shits. Pull!]

> *Friedrich conceals his presence. Paulette wants to flee*
> *with Emilie but without Karl seeing them.*

Ich brauche diese Tiere. Wer passt auf diese Pferde auf.
[I need those animals. Who is in charge of these horses?]

> *Friedrich must reveal himself before it appears strange*
> *that he hasn't.*

Friedrich (*pulling his collar up and his hat down low*)
Verwundetentransport, Herr Offizier-Stellvertreter! Die
sind nicht vom Kanonenzug, Herr Offizier-Stellvertreter.
[Transporting wounded, sir. They're not gun team, sir.]

> *Eager to get away, Friedrich begins to position Joey*
> *and Topthorn for the ambulance.*

Karl *Wer sind Sie?* [Who are you?]

Friedrich *Soldat Muller, Herr Offizier-Stellvertreter.*
[Private Muller, sir.]

Karl *Ihr Krankenwagen ist leer, Soldat. Wenn sie den*
hier ziehen können, ziehen sie auch das. Diese Kanone
müss an die Front. Spannen Sie sie vor die Kanonen
[Your ambulance is empty, Private. And if they can pull
that, they can pull this. We need to get this gun to the
front. Harness them.]

Friedrich *Befehle.* [Orders.]

Karl *Einen Krankenwagen ohne Kranke?!* [To drive an
ambulance with no men in it?!]

Friedrich *Befehle.* [Orders.]

Karl *Arschloch!* [Bastard!]

> *Karl gives up trying to get the horses.*
> *The horses play up.*

Friedrich (*to horses*) Not now, boys.

Karl *War das Englisch? Haben Sie da gerade Englisch mit ihnen geredet?* [Was that English? Did you just speak to them in English?]

Friedrich *Englisch? Nein.* [English? No.]

The ambulance is ready to go. Emilie reveals herself to the scary man.

Emilie Calm down, Joey.

Karl's ears prick up. Friedrich has also heard Emilie. He tries not to rush.

Paulette *Papiers!*

Karl *Ja, ja, ja. Sehr gut.* [Yes, yes, yes. Very good.]

Karl gives them a cursory glance.

Was war das das, kleine Mädchen? [What was that, little girl?]

He controls the placing of Paulette and Emilie – away from their escape route into the house.
Karl's got two clues about Friedrich now and he senses he might get the horses.
Friedrich's still trying not to rush, but he's flustered. Karl takes out Ned's knife and shows it to Friedrich. Paulette fears she and Emilie are caught, about to witness a horror. Exit both.

Hab ich einem Tommy abgenommen. Er hat's gezogen, ich hab's ihm reingestocken. Schon mal so ein Messer gesehen? [Took this off a Tommy. He drew it, I stuck it in him. Ever seen a knife like it?]

Friedrich Nein.

Karl leaves Friedrich alone again. Friedrich is ready to go but he's bewildered – what's Karl up to?

Karl *Worauf warten Sie?* [What are you waiting for?]

Friedrich has no choice but to leave – which is what he initially wanted, but Karl has him in disarray.

Hauptmann?

Friedrich *Ja?* [Yes?]

Karl jabs his gun at Friedrich.

Karl *Mütze ab . . . schauen Sie mich an . . . Hauptmann. Was zum Teufel geht hier vor? . . . Erklären Sie . . . wieso kämpfen Sie nicht?* [Remove your hat . . . Look at me . . . Captain. What the hell is going on? . . . Explain yourself . . . Why aren't you fighting?]

Friedrich *Es gibt keine Kavallerie mehr.* [There's no cavalry any more.]

Karl *Gibt es wohl, berittene Infanterie.* [Yes there is, they're mounted infantry.]

Friedrich *Das wusste ich nicht. Ich geh gleich und schliess mich denen an.* [I didn't know. I'll go and join them.]

Karl *Halt! Für Sie heisst es Feuerkommando!* [Stop! It's a firing squad for you!]

Friedrich *Nein! Nein, nein!* [No! No, no!]

Karl *Oder wir handeln. Du und deine Pferde ziehen meine Kanone, ja?* [Or we bargain. You and the horses pull my gun, yes?]

Friedrich looks as if he might run.

Dann mach. [Go on, then.]

Friedrich has no choice. He unhitches Joey and Topthorn and takes them to the gun team.

Feigling. Scheiss-Feigling. [Coward. Fucking coward.]

Joey and Topthorn don't want to go straight back into harness. They resist Friedrich.

Joey shows his dislike for Coco and Heine. It's reciprocated.

Friedrich harnesses the more compliant Topthorn to the gun first.

Joey still resists being harnessed.

Emilie Joey!

Karl (*to Joey*) *Ho! Ho! Geht darein!* [Harr! Harr! Get in there!]

Because Joey is leaving her, Emilie resists being taken inside by Paulette. Exit Emilie and Paulette.

Karl viciously strikes Joey, just as Ted did. Joey's response is the same: he shapes to kick Karl. Karl falls, scrabbling for his pistol. He gets up and aims.

Joey's going to get himself killed! Friedrich hurls himself in the way.

Friedrich *Sie brauchen sie doch!* [You need them!]

Karl (*pushing Friedrich*) *Aus dem Weg!* [Get out of the way!]

Friedrich (*in the way again*) *Sie brauchen sie!* [You need them!]

Karl *Ich werde schiessen! Ich werde schiessen!* [I'm going to shoot! I'm going to shoot!]

Something goes out of Friedrich.

Friedrich *Dann machen Sie doch.* [Go on, then.]

Beats.

Karl (*lowering gun*) *Spannen Sie sie vor die Kanonen.* [Harness them to the gun.]

Aber Sie haben recht. Ich brauche diese Pferde um die Kanonen zu ziehen. Und wir brauchen die Kanone um

den Krieg zu gewinnen. Spannen Sie sie ein, und los.
Vielleicht können sie den Tod an mir riechen – vor dem
Krieg war ich Metzger. Schauen Sie, hier ist ein guter
Schnitt, und hier. Hartes Fleisch allerdings. Am besten
weichkochen bevor man es röstet. Ist Muller ihr richtiger
Name? [But you are right. I need the horses to pull the
guns. And we need the gun to win the war. Hitch them
up, let's go. Perhaps they can smell death on me – I was a
butcher before the war. This is a good cut. And here. It's
tough meat, though. Better to parboil it before roasting.
Is Muller your real name?]

Friedrich *Ja.* [Yes.]

Karl *Wenn Sie versuchen abzuhauen, Muller, bring ich*
Sie um. [Try to escape, Muller, I kill you.]

TWENTY-FOUR

France: second passage of time sequence, from Christmas
1917 into 1918.

> *Soldiers – including the dead Nicholls – advance.*
> *Explosions on screen.*

> *Men die on screen.*
> *Ribs emerge from the earth.*
> *Huge poppies grow.*

> *Mud takes over.*

Joey and Topthorn's story:

> *The gun team is noticeably slowing. Coco and Heine*
> *are going so slowly that they're holding the team up.*
> *Topthorn is coughing. Karl halts the team. He and*
> *Friedrich inspect Heine and Coco. Both horses are on*

*the verge of collapse, adding to the workload. They
remove them from the harness. Then they have a very
close look at Topthorn because he is coughing.
Friedrich wills Topthorn better. Joey and Topthorn
bend and strain but the heavy gun won't move.*

Joey leads Topthorn and the gun moves.

Incoming fire from advancing British.

Coco and Heine are left behind.

*Heine makes headway, out of the scene. Coco
staggers, and falls, and is unable to rise. She seems
dead.*

Enter the carrion crow.

TWENTY-FIVE

*Territory recently vacated by Germans, October 1918.
Dusk. Silence.*

*Enter British soldiers, singly and in pairs, like wraiths
in a mist. They're hunting for the new German positions.
They're scared of finding them, and ambushes, and
booby traps. So they're as silent as possible and don't
show lights.*

They're led by Sergeant Fine.

Enter Albert and David.

Sergeant Fine Corporal?

Albert Sarge?

Sergeant Fine What d'ye think, Corporal?

Albert This horse is still warm, Sarge, so Jerry's not far
away.

David There's fresh tracks. One carriage. Deep ruts. A
gun. If this was one of their team they'll be struggling.

Sergeant Fine That gun is our target. Let's take a pause
before we catch up with them. The men are done in.

Albert I think so, Sarge.

Sergeant Fine Three minutes rest, no smoking, no lights.

Fine indicates two sentries to stand guard. The non-sentries squat rather than sit. They drink water. They lean on their rifles. They don't speak – too tired.

Sergeant Fine That gun's en route to a new firing position. Most likely against our tanks. They're only half an hour behind us, so we need to move sharpish before that gun can –

Albert Jesus!

Sergeant Fine Corporal?

Albert I thought this horse moved, Sarge.

Sergeant Fine Maybe it did.

They study Coco.

Albert Its nerves still twitching.

Sergeant Fine How are your nerves, Corporal?

Albert Good.

Sergeant Fine You've had a long war. Volunteered early on, didn't you?

Albert I'm all right, Sarge. I thought the dead horse moved, it was an honest mistake.

Sergeant Fine . . . Thought we'd lost you this morning.

Albert My lid stopped it, Sarge.

All the soldiers become alert and fan out, ready for action.
The following exchange could be gestural.

Sentry Shaw Enemy front!

Sentry Ready!

Albert Hold your fire – I think it's a child!

Sentry Shaw Hold fire!

Albert It is a child!

Emilie stops.Albert tries to bring her over, but she resists.

Jesus!

Fine approaches Emilie.

Sergeant Fine *Français? Parlez Anglais?*

Emilie shakes her head.

Ou allez? Ou chez nous?

Emilie *J'ai perdu mon cheval.*

Sergeant Fine Lost? You lost? *Perdu* is lost?

Albert She's saying she's lost her horse, Sarge.

Sergeant Fine Ask her if she's seen a Jerry gun.

Albert *Vu les Allemagnes?*

Emilie *Oui.*

Albert *Oui? Ou?*

Sergeant Fine deploys the men.

Emilie *Chez nous.*

Albert *Ou chez nous?*

Emilie *C'est plus là. J'ai perdu mon cheval.*

Albert 'S all right, 's all right, calm down.

Sergeant Fine Give her some water . . . Corporal?

Albert Sarge.

Sergeant Fine What d'ye think?

Albert Two things: one, she might have some intelligence about Jerry, and two, we can't leave her wandering about here, can we?

Sergeant Fine I agree. Three, can't take her with us, either, can we?

Albert No, Sarge.

Sergeant Fine She needs debriefing at HQ. You take her.

Albert Sarge?

Sergeant Fine You and Private Taylor. I'll fall the men in.

Albert Are you sending me back because I thought the dead horse moved?

Sergeant Fine No, I'm ordering you to escort the young *français fille* who might have intelligence because you're the best man for the job.

Albert Yes, Sarge.

Sergeant Fine Right, we go on after the gun, you go back. Deliver her safely, Corporal.

Exit all except Albert, David, Emilie.

Albert Right, then. Let's go . . .

Dead Nicholls appears to Albert.

Hang on. This horse moved again . . . She's breathing.

David What you doing?

Albert Eh, lady. You're a lady, aren't you? . . . This poor horse is not *bon*. Can you get up? . . . No? *Tres pas bon*, eh lady? . . . Distract the *français fille*, will you?

David Distract her?

Albert Don't let her see this.

He has his bayonet resting on Coco, ready to push in.

David You mental?

Albert Can't leave her like this. Stop the girl watching me.

David Eh, girl, *français. Que'lle nom?*

Albert Will you get her away from me?!

David How can I without manhandling her? She's scared enough as it is.

Albert (*to Emilie*) Stop looking – stop watching me! This isn't your horse! Your horse is lost!

Emilie curls up.

There you go. *Bon.* I'll pray for you. Free now.

(*To dead Nicholls.*) I hope he died with you. Did he die with you? I effing hope so. Sir.

He drops the picture of Joey at dead Nicholls' feet.

David Albert?

Albert (*to David*) Are you all right? Are you all right?

David Eh?

Albert leads Emilie off.

Albert Come on. Deliver her, get after Jerry.

David retrieves the picture of Joey.

David Don't you bloody well crack up on me now.

Song: 'Snowfalls' (p. 95).
An incoming German gas shell lands with a plop. David reacts first. He has his gas mask on and he urges Emilie away.

David Go! *Allez! Allez!*

Exit Emilie.
David sees Albert hasn't reacted.

Albert! Gas! . . . Narracott! Narracott! Gas! Gas mask on!

This penetrates. Albert dumbly reaches for his mask. David drags Albert off.

TWENTY-SIX

Behind new German lines. 9 November 1918.
   The gun team is halted.
   German soldiers, including Rudi (a sergeant), steal a moment's rest.

Friedrich (*to the horses*) Take the chance to play, boys. Play while the sun shines.

Rudi *Sie sprechen Englisch?* [You speak English?]

Karl *Ist das Geschirr fertig?* [That harness fixed?]

Friedrich *Fast.* [Almost.]

Karl *Beeilen Sie sich.* [Get on with it.]

Rudi *Das sind gute pferde. Viel zu gut un dieses ding hier zu ziehen.* [They're fine horses. Too fine to be pulling that thing.]

Friedrich *Die kriegen das hin. Gerade so.* [They just about manage. Just.]

Rudi Does he speak English?

Friedrich . . . No.

Karl *Was redet ihr beiden?* [What are you two saying?]

Rudi (*to Karl*) We were talking about how to win the war. *Entschuldigung. Wir reden davon wie man den Krieg gewinnt.* (*To Friedrich.*) We are retreating, aren't we?

Karl *Redet deutsch!* [Speak in German!]

Friedrich Be careful with him.

Rudi What's he going to do, shoot me?

Friedrich Yes. He would.

Rudi *Aber wir sind weiter von Paris weg als je zuvor.* [But we're further away from Paris than ever.] (*He improvises map.*) *Deutschland. Frankreich. Belgien. Die Schweiz. Die Nordsee. Wir sind hier rein, quer durch Belgien, Richtung Paris. Wir wurden gestoppt. Haben uns eingegraben. Dann ging es drei Jahre lang hin und her, mal haben wir eingesteckt, mal ausgeteilt;mal seitwaerts da hin, dann wieder dort – aber jetzt, und da gibt es keine Distussion, bewegen wir uns definitiv und unbestritten weg von Paris. Das ist ein Tuechzeug, ein grosser Rück–* [Germany. France. Belgium. Switzerland. The North Sea. We came in here, through Belgium, heading for Paris. We were stopped. We dug in. Then for three years we took a little here, gave a little there; went sideways this way, sideways that – but now, there is no argument; we are definitely, indisputably heading away from Paris. This is a retreat, a major re–]

Karl *Militärstrategie. Die Linien bleiben entlang der Front fast alle gleich, nur in manchen Gegenden machen wir von der Taktik des vorgeblichen Rückzugs Gebrauch. Täusche den Feind, lass sie vorrücken, liefere sie an die Kanonen, zermatsche sie.* [It's military strategy. The lines remain the same along most of the front, only in some areas we are using the tactic of appearing to retreat. Deceive your foe, make them advance, bring them on to your guns, crush them.]

Rudi *Ich verstehe, Herr Offizier-Stellvertreter.* [I see, sir.]

Karl *Sie verstehen? Gut.* [You see? Good.]

Rudi (*to Friedrich*) He's a Kaiser's man, all right.

Karl (*to Friedrich*) *Was hat er gerade vom Kaiser gesagt?* [What did he just say about the Kaiser?]

Friedrich *Lang lebe der Kaiser.* [Long live the Kaiser.]

Karl *Ich verstehe.* [I see.]

Rudi Those acting officers; they're the worst. Have you heard the rumours from home?

Friedrich No?

Rudi Unrest.

Friedrich What sort of unrest?

Rudi Unrest to do with wanting this war to stop.

Friedrich Unrest in Schleiden?

Rudi Unrest everywhere. They're saying we're not going to win this war. They're saying that because we attacked, we're paying for it. They're saying that we must get rid of the Kaiser and make a democracy. It would be impossible for a democracy to start a war, continue a war against the will of its people. What do you think?

Karl *Hört auf Englisch zu reden! Ich verlange zu wissen was ihr redet!* [Stop speaking English! I demand to know what you are saying!]

Joey and Topthorn play.

Friedrich (*trying to defuse*) *Schaut! Seht sie euch an, leben nur für diesen Moment. Sonnenschein, Vögel. Natur! Sie bringen euch doch auch zum Lächeln, oder? Wie Kinder, die* – [See! Look at them, just living for this instant. Sunshine, birds. Nature! They make you smile, too, you see? Like children, they –]

Joey sees Topthorn is panting. His breath is short and rasping. Topthorn falls. He lifts his head to look at Joey.

Topthorn lies still. Joey is distressed.
Friedrich listens at Topthorn's chest.
The others crowd around.

Er ist tot, verdammt nochmal. [He's dead, for God's sake.]

Rudi *Kannst du nichts machen, mein Freund.* [Nothing you can do, my friend.]

Joey is making movements that suggest he's trying to revive Topthorn.

Friedrich We killed you.

Rudi He's out of the war; that's something.

Friedrich I was going to take you home . . . Noble, noble cavalry horse. First Siegfried, now you . . . *Verdammt sei der Krieg. Verdammt sei der Scheiss-Kaiser.* [Damn this war! Damn the fucking Kaiser!]

Karl *Verdammt sei der Scheiss-Kaiser?* [Damn the fucking Kaiser?!]

Suddenly an incoming shell lands nearby. Everybody reacts except Joey and Friedrich. Karl is badly hurt by shrapnel.
Another incoming shell. Then a new and terrible sound. A rumbling and a squeaking, a grating and a roaring.
Enter Schmidt, fleeing from the direction of the rumbling, squeaking, grating, roaring.

Schmidt *Es kommt! Es kommt!* [It's coming! It's coming!]

Exit Schmidt and all except Joey, Friedrich, Rudi.
Friedrich tries to drag Joey away, but Joey won't budge from Topthorn.
Rudi tries to drag Friedrich away, but Friedrich doesn't move. Exit Rudi.

Hanz Hurry! Hurry!

*The terrible sound is getting closer. Joey turns his head
to listen, and puts himself between it and Topthorn.*
    *Friedrich deliberately approaches the tank. Its
machine guns fire, hitting him.*

Friedrich Little Gisa!

Friedrich dies.
    Joey can't believe it.
    Joey returns to Topthorn as if to say 'Get up!'
    *Joey whinnies to Topthorn as if to say 'Get up and
let's get out of here!'*
    *Then the rumbling, squeaking starts up again,
getting louder, and louder . . .*
    Joey stands guard over Topthorn.
    *A British tank bursts into view and rolls towards
them.*
    *Joey flinches and retreats a few steps, then returns
to Topthorn, and faces the tank.*
    There's a stand-off.
    Joey doesn't budge.
    The tank advances.
    Joey doesn't budge.
    The tank's gun is brought to bear on Joey.
    Joey flees.

TWENTY-SEVEN

*Joey's night. End of October into the beginning of
November 1918.*
    For the first time ever in his life, Joey's alone . . .
    He runs.
    He crosses a river.
    He gallops through a farmyard.

He jumps fences. He jumps ditches.
He clatters through a deserted village.
He finds a stream. He drinks.
Night comes. He dozes standing up.
He's woken by a white flare.
A machine gun chatters into life.
Joey runs again, in the dark.
He stumbles.
He runs into barbed wire.
He screams.
His efforts to free himself worsen his injuries.
Eventually, he breaks free.
He's limping, in pain.
A battle starts up next to him in the dark.
He tries to limp away from it, but it breaks out in that direction, too.
Every way he tries to limp, the battle breaks out.
He's in the middle of it, with nowhere to run.
Joey stands still. Above and around him tracer flickers; lines of red and white and yellow and green. All around him are muzzle flashes, and the flares of explosions.
Joey sways. He might fall.
If he falls he might never rise again.
Suddenly everything stops, the war stops.
Joey doesn't change but around him appears a mist.

TWENTY-EIGHT

No man's land. 10 November 1918.
We begin to realise that Joey is between opposing positions (not necessarily trenches at this stage of the war) – Germans on one side, British on the other.
A Geordie sentry, Geordie, glimpses Joey.

Geordie Stand to! Stand to!

Sergeant Thunder (*now a Regimental Sergeant-Major*) What is it, Geordie?

Geordie I saw something moving in no man's land.

Sergeant Thunder What was it? The whole effing German army or just one or two of them out for a pre-breakfast stroll?

Geordie Wasn't a man, Sarge – looked more like a horse or a cow to me.

Sergeant Thunder A cow or a horse? Your eyes are playing tricks on you – or perhaps you think it's an effing Trojan horse, or a Trojan cow, an elaborate ploy by Jerry to –

Geordie Honest, Sarge, I saw it.

Sergeant Thunder Well, I can't see anything, and that's because there's nothing there. You're all of a jitter, Geordie, and you've gone and woken everyone up because you thought you saw an effing quadruped. But now we're here, and there's a London pea-souper out there, I want you to keep your eyes peeled for Germans, trez beans? Toot sweet, an' all.

Geordie I did see it, Sarge.

Sergeant Thunder There'll be a rum ration in a minute, Geordie. After that you might see all sorts in that mist. Perhaps an effing cow will jump over an effing moon.

Manfred, a German in the opposing line, glimpses Joey.

Manfred *Achtung! Schnell!*

Ludwig *Was ist los?*

Manfred *Ein Pferd!*

Ludwig *Ein was?*

Joey is clearly visible.

Manfred *Ein Pferd!*

Geordie There! I told you – there is a horse!

Sergeant Thunder Well, eff me. How the eff did that get there?

A few beats, then both sides begin to call to Joey.
He's swayed one way, whereupon the 'losing' side redoubles its efforts. He goes towards them and the same happens. Both sides very much want him to come to them.

Geordie Listen to the lads, Sarge. They want him. And look, there's a white flag.

Manfred is waving it, and tentatively climbing out of his position.

Sergeant Thunder Hold your fire!

Geordie *(fashioning a white flag)* Jerry's going for him!

Sergeant Thunder Are you sure about this, Geordie?

Geordie We can't just let the effing Jerries effing have him.

Sergeant Thunder Too effing right, Geordie.

Geordie climbs out, too.

Ludwig *Nicht stiessen!* [Don't shoot!]

Sergeant Thunder Hold fire, but be prepared!

Joey shows a bit more interest now that two men are approaching.

Manfred *(with noises) Kam, her.*

Men from both trenches call to Joey.

Geordie Hey, bonny lad!

Manfred *Her, hierher.*

Geordie Eh, Dobbin – you're going the wrong way, see.

Manfred and Geordie arrive at him. They study each other for a few moments. It's tense.

Manfred Horse?

Geordie Yes . . . *Pferd?*

Manfred *Ja.*

They concentrate on Joey. Help him. This is a novel sight for their comrades – enemies co-operating. A quiet descends.

Manfred *Alles ist still.* [Everyone has gone quiet.]

Geordie We must be careful not to start a war, eh?

Manfred *Was?* [What?]

Geordie Nothing.

Manfred *Er hat viel Blut verloren.* [He has lost a lot of blood.]

Geordie He needs a veterinarian.

Manfred *Was war das?* [Say again?]

Geordie A veterinarian, he needs a –

Manfred *Ah ja. Veterinär. Ja, die haben wir.* [Ah, yes. Vetenirär. Yes, we have them.]

Geordie How do we decide who takes him, then?

Manfred .

Heads or tails?

Manfred *Kopf oder Zahl .* [Heads or tails.]

Geordie This is heads, this tails.

Manfred *Kopf. Zahl. Diese Muenze ist wie das Pferd..ich werfe, du rufst, ja?* [The coin is like the horse . . . I toss, you call, yes?]

> *Manfred holds the coin aloft and turns a full circle so both sides can see it. There are shouts of encouragement from both sides. Then silence. Manfred flips the coin.*

Geordie *Kopf!*

> *Manfred shows Geordie the result.*
>   *When Geordie leads Joey the cheers explode on the British side.*

Manfred *Bon chance. Auf Wiedersehen.*

Geordie Same to you, man.

> *When Manfred hands Geordie the reigns, cheers explode on the British side.*

Sergeant Thunder Trez beans, Geordie, trez beans!

> *Joey lets Geordie lead him.*
>   *Song: 'Brisk Young Ploughboy' (p. 96).*

TWENTY-NINE

Behind British lines. 11 November 1918 – Armistice Day.
  A chaotic clearing station. Wounded men and horses being attended to.
  Enter Albert, blinded, eyes bandaged, being led by David.
  Enter Major Callaghan.

Callaghan Gas?

David Yes, Major.

Callaghan (*examines Albert*) Are you totally blind?

David No, sir. He can see still shapes.

Callaghan It was only tear gas. You're lucky. You will recover your sight..

David That's good, Albert.

Callaghan You'll be all right.

Albert Oh aye! Am I? Am I all right?

Callaghan What do you mean by that reply, Corporal? . . . Where was your gas mask, Corporal?

David It was damaged, sir.

Callaghan It's not dangerous, and it's not a Blighty one. Category two: slight. Wait there for an orderly.

David Albert, snap out of it.

Enter Joey with Sergeant Thunder and Geordie.
Cheers from soldiers as they enter.

Sergeant Thunder This, sir, is the no man's land horse, sir.

Geordie It's just his leg, as far as we can see.

Martin It needs cleaning out, straight away.

Geordie We sluiced it with water, sir, but we didn't try anything else.

Martin You did the right thing. Water, please.

Sergeant Thunder Ordinarily we wouldn't be making such a fuss over an injured horse, Major, but the men have got it into their heads that he's special.

Martin He looks as if he was a fine animal once.

Geordie We didn't feed him in case he needs an operation.

Martin An operation? He'll be lucky.

Medical supplies are brought and employed. Sergeant Thunder crosses to David and Albert.

Sergeant Thunder (*to Albert and David*) I know you, don't I?

David It was when we disembarked, Sergeant.

Sergeant Thunder When?

David March 1915, Sergeant.

Sergeant Thunder You've done well (*to stay alive*). What's he got?

David Tear gas, Sergeant.

Sergeant Thunder It'll wear off . . . I said it'll wear off . . . Corporal? Are you all right, Corporal?

David He's just a bit tired, Sergeant.

Sergeant Thunder What's his name?

David Corporal Narracott, Sergeant.

Sergeant Thunder Narracott . . . Eff me, I remember you. You were the one badgering me about effing horses . . . Corporal? That was you, wasn't it?

Martin It's no use. (*He checks revolver.*)

Taff Hear that, Sarge? It's no use.

Sergeant Thunder That's a shame, that's a damn shame, sir. The men are talking about him as if he's some sort of miracle.

Martin He's half dead and I've got no one to look after him.

David They're going to help a horse, Albert, like you helped that German one.

Albert Off him? Good. Poor lad.

David That's right, Albert. Poor lad.

Martin aims at Joey.

Albert I had a horse once.

David Yes, Albert; I know you did.

Albert Joey, he was called.

David I know.

Albert Joey. Joey.

Joey reacts a little to Albert's voice.

David Shush, Albert.

Martin pulls trigger. The gun fails to fire.

Martin For God's sake! Gun jammed. Sergeant.

Sergeant Thunder lends his rifle.

Albert Joey. Joey.

Joey reacts more to Albert's voice.

Martin What's going on over there?

David Shut it, Albert.

Martin He's upsetting this horse. Get him away from here, that's an order!

Sergeant Thunder Get him away, Private. This is bad enough without –

Albert What does he mean, I'm upsetting this horse? What horse?

David Shush, Albert, we've been ordered away –

Albert (*tearing off bandages*) The one he's about to off? Is he answering? Is the *bon* horse answering to Joey?

Joey responds more. Thunder spots this and perhaps closes on Martin and Joey.
   Martin aims.

Joey! Joey boy!

Joey wants to go to Albert.

Sergeant Thunder Sir, don't pull the trigger –

Martin What?

Albert Don't off him! Don't off the *bon* horse! Joey! Joey!

Joey definitely reacts, taking steps towards Albert.

Sergeant Thunder Do you see that?

Martin What on earth?

Albert Joey? Joey boy, is it you?

Joey walks. He and Albert meet up with each other.

Sergeant Thunder It's his effing horse sir. His effing horse from effing home.

Albert's Devon accent comes back up a few notches.

Albert Hello, Joey. Hello, boy. Where you bin, then? Where you bin? What a dance, what a dance you've led me. Good boy. Good boy. Does that hurt? Sorry, Joey, sorry. You've bin in the bliddin' wars, haven't you? We'll mend that, we will, we will. We'll mend that. Oh Joey. You're alive, you're alive, you're alive . . . Good boy. Good boy. Well done. What a *bon* boy. *Trez bon*, Joey. *Trez bon*. Am I all right? Am I all right? Too effing right I am, too effing right. Oh Joey . . .

A bell chimes eleven times, signalling the end of the war. The other men react in various ways. Some kneel, some have their head in their hands, some embrace,

86

some just want to be alone. Not one of them jumps up and down shouting 'Yes!' or anything like that.

David That's it.

Albert (*now sighted*) We've made it.

David Thanks, Albert . . . I've got something of yours.

Albert Oh?

David You dropped this (*the picture of Joey*).

Albert Thank you, David.

David Thank you.

Exit all except Joey and Albert.
If we haven't seen them galloping together yet, it should occur here.

THIRTY

Narracott's farm. Dawn. Birdsong. Perhaps Goose is there.
Enter Rose, rubbing her eyes.
Joey and Albert amble towards her, the slanting sun behind them.

Rose Eh?

Ted What is it?

Rose A man, and a horse . . . It can't be –

Rose picks up her skirts and runs towards Joey and Albert. Ted celebrates.
The End.

War Horse Songbook

JOHN TAMS

The Devonshire Carol

The lambkin in the manger
The light upon the lea
The moorland yields to glory
The shepherds bend the knee
And all are wrapped in grace
And all are gifted mirth
Peace walks upon this blessèd land
Peace walks upon this blessèd land
Peace walks upon this blessèd land
Goodwill upon all earth

The ploughboy and his traces
The line upon the land
All's gift by nature's graces
Her bounty to command
And all are wrapped in grace
And all are gifted mirth
Peace walks upon this blessèd land
Peace walks upon this blessèd land
Peace walks upon this blessèd land
Goodwill upon all earth

Tommy in the meadow
Tommy in the byre
Tommy on the firestep
Tommy on the wire
And those who walked in war
And those who walked in peace
And those who walked this blessèd land
And those who walked this blessèd land
And those who walked this blessèd land
Their souls shall never cease

And those we leave behind us
Those who count the cost
Their future is provided
By those who won and lost
And those who walked in joy
And those who cherished peace
And those who walked this blessèd land
And those who walked this blessèd land
And those who walked this blessèd land
Their souls shall never cease

Only Remembered

Fading away like the stars in the morning
Losing their light in the glorious sun
Thus shall we pass from this earth and its toiling
Only remembered for what we have done
Only remembered, only remembered
Only remembered for what we have done
Thus shall we pass from this earth and its toiling
Only remembered for what we have done

Horses and men – ploughshares and traces
The line on the land – the paths of the sun
Season by season we mark nature's graces
Only remembered for what we have done
Only remembered, only remembered
Only remembered for what we have done
Season by season we mark nature's graces
Only remembered for what we have done

Who'll sing the anthems and who'll tell the story?
Will the line hold, will it scatter and run?
Shall we at last be united in glory?
Only remembered for what we have done
Only remembered, only remembered,
Only remembered for what we have done
Shall we at last be united in glory?
Only remembered for what we have done
Only remembered for what we have done

The Scarlet and the Blue

Then hoorah for the Scarlet and the Blue
With the helmets a-glittering in the sun
And the bayonets flash like lightening
To the beating of a military drum
And no more will I go harvesting
Or gathering the golden corn
For I've took the good King's shilling
And I'm off tomorrow morn

Snowfalls

Cruel winter cuts through like the reaper
The old year lies withered and slain
And like Barleycorn who rose from the grave
A new year will rise up again

CHORUS

And the snow falls
The wind calls
And the year turns round again
And like Barleycorn who rose from the grave
A new year will rise up again

And I'll wager a hat full of guineas
Against all of the songs you can sing
Some day you'll love and the next day you'll lose,
A winter will turn into spring

CHORUS

Phoebe arise
A gleam in her eyes
And the year turns round again
And like Barleycorn who rose from the grave
A new year will rise up again

But there will come a time of great plenty
A time of good harvest and sun
Till then put your trust in tomorrow my friend
For yesterday's over and done

CHORUS

Ploughed, sown,
Reaped and mown
And the year turns round again
And like Barleycorn who rose from the grave
A new year will rise up again

Brisk Young Ploughboy

It is of a brisk young ploughboy, a-ploughing on
    the plain
And his horse it stood down in yonder shade
It was down in yonder glade he went whistling
    to plough
And by chance there he met a pretty maid,
A pretty maid
And by chance there he met a pretty maid

And oft-times he ventured unto that yonder glade
And contented they lay amidst the shade
And the sweet bells they did ring and the
    nightingales did sing
All for the ploughboy and his tender maid
Tender maid
All for the ploughboy and his tender maid

So when her aged parents they did come to know
That her love he was a-ploughing on the plain
They sent for the press-gang
And pressed her love away
They sent him to the war to be slain,
To be slain
They sent him to the war to be slain

He has written home a letter the best that he
    knew how
Saying this cruel war shall ne'er keep us apart
While cannon loudly roar I shall keep our love
    secure
For my tunic button's tight around your heart
Around your heart
For my tunic button's tight around your heart

Rolling Home

Round goes the wheel of fortune
Don't be afraid to ride
There's a land of milk and honey
Waits on the other side
There'll be peace and there'll be plenty
You'll never need to roam
When we go rolling home,
  when we go rolling home

CHORUS

Rolling home,
When we go rolling home
When we go rolling, rolling
When we go rolling home

The gentry in their fine array
Do prosper night and morn
While we unto the fields must go
To plough and sow the corn
The rich may steal the power
But the glory's ours alone
When we go rolling home,
  when we go rolling home

CHORUS

The summer of resentment
The winter of despair
The journey to contentment
Is set with trap and snare
Stand true and stand together
Your labour is your own
When we go rolling home,
  when we go rolling home

So pass the bottle round
And let the toast go free
Here's a health to every labourer
Wherever they may be
Fair wages now and ever
Let's reap what we have sown
When we go rolling,
  when we go rolling home

CHORUS

Stand To

Stand to me bonny lads
Stand to and make you ready
Stand to me bonny lads
Hold the line right steady
Let pride burn through the flame
This day shall bear your name
Stand to me bonny lads –
  hold the line right steady

Goodbye Dolly Gray

Goodbye Dolly I must leave you
Though it breaks my heart to go
Something tells me I am needed
At the front to fight the foe
See the soldier boys are marching
And I can no longer stay
Hark, I hear the bugle calling
Goodbye Dolly Gray